Ride Your Bike

Contents

How to use this guide

The *Ride Your Bike* guides are designed for riders of all levels: from complete novices and those with a little experience to people that have been cycling all their lives.

Chapter 1 aims to whet the appetite for the area covered by the guide. As well as general information about the geological character and history of the region, places of interest are identified and described.

Chapter 2 provides important basic information on preparing yourself and your bike before a ride, getting to the start of a route, navigation skills, as well as advice on safety and emergencies.

If you would like to know more about bikes, equipment, repair and maintenance and travelling further afield into Europe and the rest of the world, *Mountain Biking, The Bike Book* and *Fix Your Bike* are published by Haynes and available from all good bike and bookshops.

A locator map is included on pages 4-5 for easy identification of rides in your area. The ride facts chart at the back of the guide is designed to provide key information 'at a glance' to make selecting a ride that suits your mood, energy level and degree of expertise simple and quick.

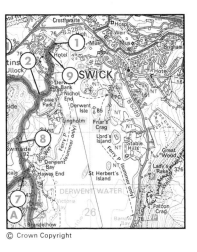

© Crown Copyright

The guide contains 19 rides graded easy, medium and difficult.

Easy rides are for novices, families with young children and for people who are getting back into riding after a gap. They are relatively short and use good surfaces such as dismantled railways. You don't need any expertise to do these rides, just the enthusiasm to get out there.

Medium rides are a little more challenging in terms of distance and terrain. If you have done all the easy routes, have built up some confidence and mastered the basic trail techniques try one of the shorter routes in this category. You will soon feel able to try the rest. Check through the directions to alert yourself to anything you may not be able to manage.

Difficult rides are for the experienced mountain biker and demand a good command of trail techniques, fitness and more than a dash of courage. They are exciting and challenging and great fun. Make sure you and your bike are in good shape before you contemplate a difficult route: they often go into remote areas and use challenging terrain.

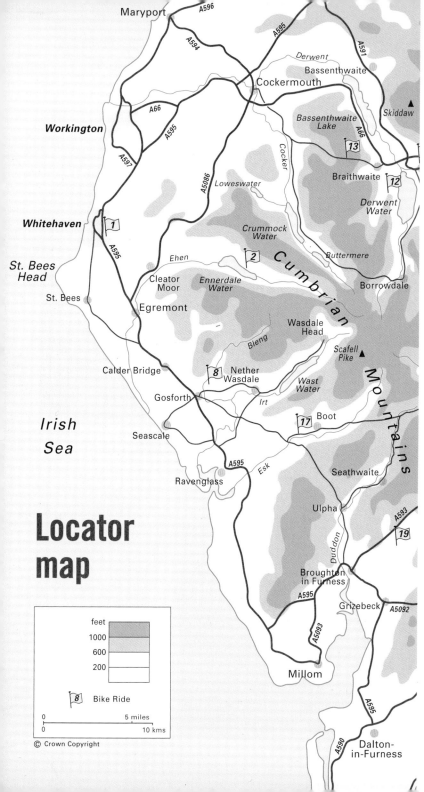

Locator
map

Maryport

A596

A595

A594

Derwent

Bassenthwaite

Cockermouth

A595

A591

Skiddaw

Bassenthwaite Lake

A66

A66

Workington

Cocker

13

A595

Braithwaite

12

A597

A5086

Loweswater

Derwent Water

Whitehaven

1

Crummock Water

Cumbrian

Buttermere

St. Bees Head

A595

Ehen

Borrowdale

St. Bees

Cleator Moor

Ennerdale Water

Egremont

Wasdale Head

Bleng

Scafell Pike

Mountains

Irish Sea

Calder Bridge

8

Nether Wasdale

Wast Water

Gosforth

Irt

17

Boot

Seascale

Seathwaite

A595

Esk

Ravenglass

Ulpha

A593

19

Duddon

Broughton in Furness

A595

Grizebeck

A5092

A5093

Millom

A595

A590

Dalton-in-Furness

feet	
1000	
600	
200	

8 Bike Ride

0   5 miles
0   10 kms

© Crown Copyright

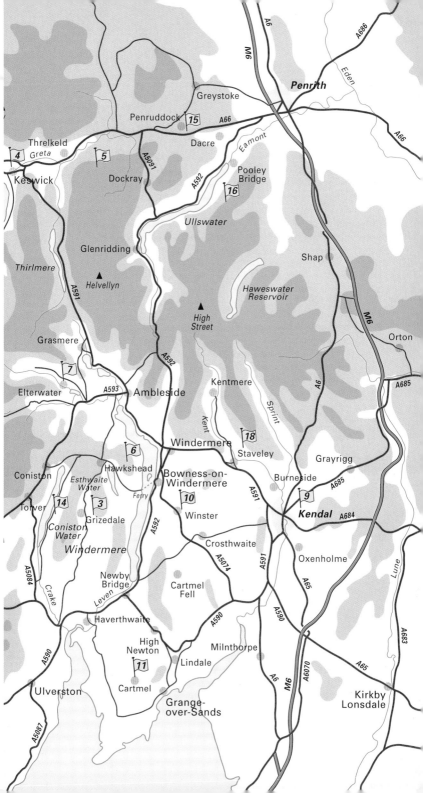

Chapter 1: Introduction to the area

F EW AREAS CAN BOAST so much natural beauty condensed in such a small area. Draw a line 20 miles around Grasmere and you have encircled the National Park. Within its boundaries the forces of man and nature have combined over thousands of years to produce a landscape of lofty crags and summits towering over blue lakes and also gentler scenes of buttercup-filled pastures grazed by sheep and bounded by drystone walls built generations ago. In the valleys stand solid stone farmhouses often whitewashed and slate-roofed and the whole area is criss-crossed by rights of way giving access to all those who wish to explore its secrets and enjoy its challenges.

The islands of Derwent Water from beneath Cat Bells

For the cyclist, the Lake District provides a whole range of options: for the beginner there are the converted dismantled railways at Whitehaven and Keswick and the waymarked trails of the large Forestry Commission holdings at Grizedale, Whinlatter and

Ennerdale; the network of C roads and unclassified roads, particularly between Lake Windermere and the M6, is an unsung delight; and as for off-road mountain bike challenges, you could carry your bike to the top of Skiddaw, Esk Hause, Sty Head, High Street and Helvellyn but you would probably have to carry it down again. This guide limits itself to off-road routes which can be ridden along most of their course and at worst will involve short sections of pushing. That still leaves plenty of options around the edges of the central fells. Add to that the 259-mile Cumbria Cycle Way which uses quiet roads around the perimeter of the county and the Sustrans Sea to Sea Cycle Route which passes through Cumbria on its way over the Pennines to the North Sea, and you have a variety of cycle rides to suit every taste and degree of fitness.

A fine stone bridleway above Ullswater

The Northern Lakes and North Cumbria

T HE BULK OF Blencathra and Skiddaw dominate this area. Skiddaw is one of the four mountains that rise to over 913 metres (3000 ft) in the Lake District. Nevertheless, Blencathra is the more striking of the two peaks with a very pronounced 'saddleback' ridge that is visible from many miles around. Penrith is well-placed for exploring both the Lake District and the Eden Valley, which has a network of quiet lanes either side of the majestic River Eden. The northern

Whinlatter Forest, beneath Seat How

lakes, Bassenthwaite, Derwent Water, Thirlmere, Ullswater and Haweswater, all have rideable lakeside tracks or quiet lanes from which to appreciate their beauty.

Keswick, capital of the northern lakes, is one of the main tourist centres of the Lake District and a good base for rides in all directions, though it does get very busy in the summer. North of the National Park is a vast area of quiet lanes stretching as far as the Solway Firth. Little visited, it offers countless miles of easy cycling on flat lanes with very little traffic. Of particular note is the lane that runs along the coast of the Solway Firth through Bowness-on-Solway with fine views across to Scotland.

The clock tower in Keswick High Street

Places to visit

Fairytale façades of towers, turrets and battlements are the only remnants of the 19th-century castle in **Lowther** which was demolished in 1957. **Lowther Park** was created in 1283 for the estate's deer and is now a country park with nature trails, children's entertainments, rare breeds and red deer. The poets **Coleridge** and **Southey** lived in **Keswick** which has several museums with a variety of displays including a relief model of the Lake District and works by the Lakeland poets. **Castlerigg Stone Circle** is a Bronze Age ring of stones probably 3500 years old standing up to 1.8m (6ft) tall set in an amphitheatre of hills. A short walk from the carpark on Ullswater shore leads to **Aira Force** where **Aira Beck** rushes under a stone bridge and pours 21m (70ft) down a green hole.

Rides in this area featured in the book: Keswick Railway Path, Keswick Coach Road, Greystoke, Whinlatter Forest, Askham Fell, Derwent Water

East of Lake Windermere

IT IS EASY TO DIVIDE this area in two: to the north rise the mountains of Harter Fell and High Street, named after the old Roman Road which used to pass right over the mountain and link Penrith with Windermere. Just three dead-end roads penetrate deep into these hills along the valleys of Longsleddale, Kentmere and Troutbeck/Hagg Gill. To the south, within a 10-mile radius of Kendal, there is an astonishing network of small lanes, carrying very little traffic and ideal for year-round cycling. Here is a more intimate beauty of outlying farms and hamlets, broadleaf woodlands, rivers and streams and the occasional rocky outcrop in an otherwise rolling green countryside grazed by livestock and marked by drystone walls.

View to the east of Stile End Farm

A steep climb over Stile End before the longer climb to Garburn

Places to visit

Windermere is the longest lake in England and nearby you will find the Steamboat Museum and the National Park Visitor Centre. This is Beatrix Potter country and Bowness-on-Windermere hosts the **World of Beatrix Potter** exhibition including a 3-D tableaux, music and videos. The elegant 18th-century Abbot Hall in **Kendal** preserves local traditions in the Museum of Lakeland Life and Industry. The Great Hall of **Levens Hall** was started in 1250, but most of it is Elizabethan. The garden is full of curious shapes of fantastic 17th-century topiary maintained in their original form. The 17th-century **Holker Hall** is a former residence of the Dukes of Devonshire. Woodcarvings by local craftsmen, period furniture and paintings, a deer park and an exhibition of period kitchens are among the attractions.

Rides in this area featured in the book: Quiet lanes north of Kendal, Quiet lanes south of Windermere, Quiet lanes north of Cartmel, Garburn Pass

Grizedale and Furness

T HIS AREA OFFERS THE BEST easy offroad cycling in the Lake District, some of its finest views and has the advantage of being relatively close to the M6. Access is via one of three routes - the A590, Ambleside, or, more environmentally sound and certainly more scenic and adventurous, the ferry across Lake Windermere from Bowness. In the centre of the area lies Grizedale Forest, the largest forestry holding in the Lake District and also the most developed for recreational cycling. Ambleside, Grasmere and the Langdales represent the hub of tourism in the heart of the Lake District and their popularity and the resulting weight of traffic makes cycling difficult during busy periods. Out of season during the week many more options are open. To the west lies the beautiful Duddon Valley and to the south lie the old town and port of Ulverston and the shipbuilding yards of Barrow-in-Furness.

The bridleway east of Coniston Water

Places to visit

Hawkshead is a medieval village with an intricate maze of alleys. William Heelis worked in Thrimble Hall when he married Beatrix Potter and it now houses an exhibition of her life and work. The poet **William Wordsworth** lived in Dove Cottage, Grasmere from 1799 to 1808. He is buried in the village churchyard along with his family. The Grasmere and Wordsworth Museum nearby holds manuscripts and relics. **Hill Top** is the 17th-century farm that inspired Beatrix Potter's work. It was bought as her retreat in 1905 and is now preserved by the National Trust. The old town and port of **Ulverston** is where comedian **Stan Laurel** was born in 1890; the **Laurel and Hardy Museum** contains press cuttings, personal possessions and film archive. **Coniston** is a village dominated by the craggy Old Man of Coniston, towering 790m (2635ft) high. Take a ride on the lake on **Gondola**, a stately steam yacht first launched in 1859. The **Ruskin Museum** describes the life and work of the Victorian artist with paintings, drawings and personal items.

The junction at Hall Dunnerdale in the Duddon Valley

Rides in this area featured in the book: Grizedale Forest, Claife Heights, Elterwater, Coniston Water Woodland Fell to the Duddon Valley

The West Coast to the Fells

THE COAST OF CUMBRIA is a complete contrast to the timeless beauty of the Lake District. The area developed as a result of mining, ironworks and shipbuilding and now all these heavy industries are gone and the towns of Whitehaven and Workington are coming to terms with the post-industrial age. The nuclear power station at Sellafield provides many of the jobs in the area and is trying hard to attract tourists.

Within the National Park, Eskdale is a delight; forestry trails through Blengdale Forest and Ennerdale Forest offer fine year-round offroad tracks. Wast Water is the deepest and most darkly brooding of all the lakes in the region and the setting of the Wasdale Head Inn in the very heart of the central fells is one of the most outstanding in the whole of the Lake District.

A carpet of daisies and buttercups in Eskdale

Places to visit

Ravenglass is a seafaring village and the site of a 4-acre Roman fort with a bathhouse. The century-old miniature railway takes tourists on a scenic seven-mile trip up Eskdale. **St Bees**, named after St Bee or St Bega, thought to be an Irish princess who established a nunnery there, lies in the valley south of St Bees Head whose sandstone cliffs rise to 150m (500ft) above the shore. Sea birds include kittiwakes, fulmars and black guillemots. **Wasdale Head** is a hamlet at the head of dramatic **Wast Water**, the deepest Lakeland lake at 77m (258ft). It is a centre for climbing on Great Gable, Kirk Fell, Yewbarrow, and **Scafell Pike**, England's highest peak at 963m (3210ft). The Poet, **William Wordsworth** was born in **Cockermouth** in a Georgian house at the end of the main street. There are remains of a 14th-century castle where the River Cocker and the River Derwent meet and also a Toy and Doll museum.

Across Ennerdale Water to Iron Crag and Caw Fell

Rides in this area featured in the book: Eskdale, Ennerdale Forest, Blengdale Forest, Whitehaven to Rowrah

Local amenities

For up-to-date information about accommodation (including a booking service), places to visit, public transport timetables and local events, Tourist Information Centres and National Park Information Centres offer an excellent service. An asterisk indicates that the centre is not open all year round. See pages 18-19 for their location. Also given below are some cycle hire companies although the local Information Centres will have the most up-to-date information on where to hire bicycles.

*Ambleside
Old Courthouse, Church Street,
Ambleside, Cumbria LA22 0BT
Tel: 015394 32582

*Bowness-on-Windermere
Glebe Road, Bowness-on- Windermere,
Cumbria LA23 3HJ
Tel: 015394 42895

Cockermouth
Town Hall, Market Street,
Cockermouth, Cumbria CA13 9NP
Tel: 01900 822634

*Coniston
Ruskin Avenue, Coniston,
Cumbria LA21 8EH
Tel: 015394 41533

Egremont
12 Main Street, Egremont,
Cumbria CA22 2DW
Tel: 01946 820693

*Glenridding
Ullswater Information Centre,
Main carpark, Glenridding, Penrith,
Cumbria CA11 0PA
Tel: 017684 82414

*Grasmere
Redbank Road, Grasmere,
Cumbria LA22 9SW
Tel: 015394 35245

*Hawkshead
Main carpark, Hawkshead,
Cumbria LA22 0NT
Tel: 015394 36525

Kendal
Town Hall, Highgate, Kendal,
Cumbria LA9 4DL
Tel: 01539 725758

Keswick
Moot Hall, Market Square,
Keswick, Cumbria CA12 4JR
Tel: 017687 72645

Penrith
Robinson's School, Middlegate,
Penrith, Cumbria CA11 7PT
Tel: 01768 867466

*Pooley Bridge
The Square, Pooley Bridge,
Cumbria CA10 2NP
Tel: 017684 86530

*Ravenglass
Ravenglass and Eskdale Railway,
Ravenglass, Cumbria CA18 1SW
Tel: 01229 717278

*Seatoller
Seatoller Barn, Borrowdale,
Keswick, Cumbria CA12 5XN
Tel: 017687 77294

Ulverston
Coronation Hall, County Square,
Ulverston, Cumbria LA12 7LZ
Tel: 01229 587120

Whitehaven
Market Hall, Market Place,
Whitehaven, Cumbria CA28 7JG
Tel: 01946 695678

Windermere
Victoria Street, Windermere,
Cumbria Windermere LA23 1AD
Tel: 015394 46499

*not open all year round

Cycle Hire

Ambleside
Ambleside Mountain Bikes Ghyllside
Cycles, The Slack, Ambleside, LA22 9DQ
Tel: 015394 33592

Appleby-in-Westmorland
Eden Bikes
The Sands, Appleby-in-Westmorland,
Cumbria CA16 6XR
Tel: 017683 53533

Grizedale
Old Hall Carpark,
Grizedale Forest Park Centre, nr.
Hawkshead, Cumbria LA22 0QJ
Tel: 01229 860369

Keswick
Keswick Mountain Bikes
Southey Hill, Keswick CA12 5ND
Tel: 017687 75202

Kirkby Stephen
Mortlake Mountain Bikes
32 & 34 Market Street,
Kirkby Stephen, Cumbria CA17 4QW
Tel: 017683 71666/71993
(for booking after shop hours)

Penrith
Eden Cyclo-Tours
Unit 8, Redhills Business Park,
Penrith, Cumbria CA11 0DL
Tel: 01768 899950

Talkin Tarn Country Park,
Brampton, Cumbria CA8 1HN
Tel: 01697 73129

Windermere
Ashton's Cycle
12 Main Road, Windermere,
Cumbria
Tel: 015394 47779

Lakeland Leisure, Not Just a Bike Shop
Lake Road, Bowness on Windemere,
Cumbria LA23 3BJ
Tel: 015394 44786

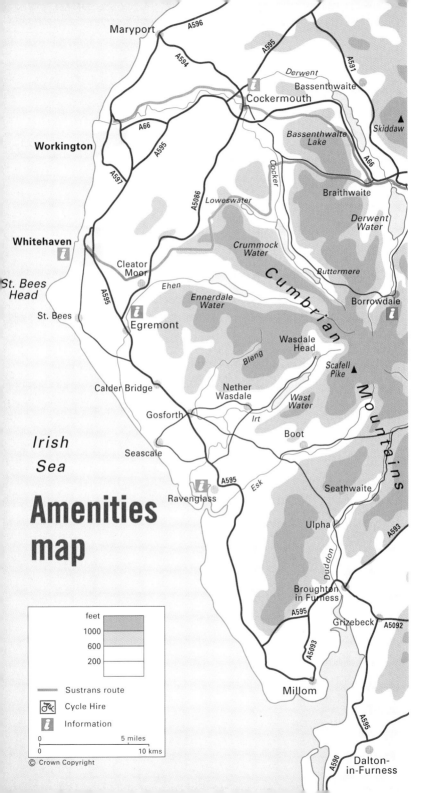

Amenities map

Irish Sea

feet

1000
600
200

— Sustrans route

🚴 Cycle Hire

ℹ️ Information

0 — 5 miles
0 — 10 kms

© Crown Copyright

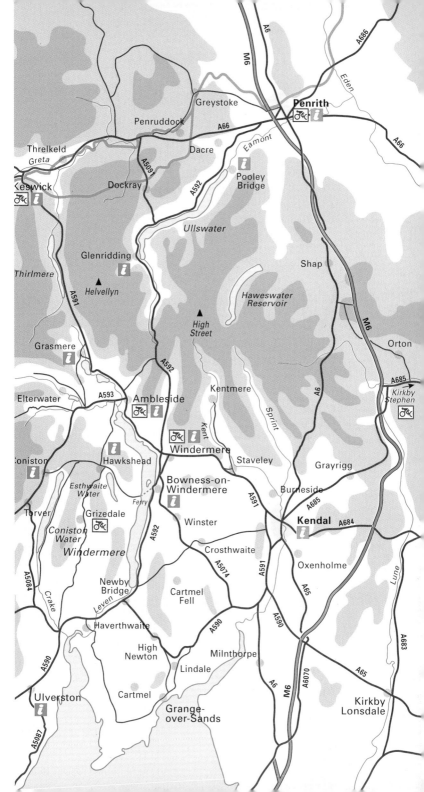

Weather and seasons

The weather can change very quickly in the Lake District, even on fine summer days, so be prepared for rain and a big drop in temperature and carry spare warm and waterproof clothing. A sudden deterioration in visibility is also possible. It is useful to have a compass at all times both for navigation in poor visibility and for cycling in woodland or Forestry Commission holdings where there are no waymarkings. The problems in summer are more likely to revolve around crowded trails: courtesy and common sense are vital if you are sharing busy trails with walkers and other cyclists.

Trails

The tracks and bridleways of the Lake District are certainly slower and more difficult in the winter but almost all are rideable. From an environmental viewpoint it is not a good idea to go across open moorland or soft grass when the ground is waterlogged because of the damage done to the fragile vegetation and the opening up of furrows down which water can run and erode the earth back to rock.

Cowparsley and cranesbill on the lanes above Ullswater

The worst problem you are likely to encounter in the summer months is the amount of other people using the trails. If at all possible avoid Easter, Bank Holidays and school half-terms. Riding during the week in May and June or from mid-September to the end of October is probably the best time of all.

Winter

Days are much shorter in the winter, particularly this far north, so plan to have your ride finished by early to mid-afternoon. Don't be too ambitious: many accidents happen when people are determined to stick to a pre-set plan and fail to alter their intended route to take account of the prevailing weather conditions. Having everything ready and getting an early start is essential in the winter.

Bright clothing and lights will help you to be located in the event of an accident and are vital on roads on those dark winter days when it never really seems to get light.

Forecasts

Weather forecasts vary considerably in accuracy; often the local forecast is very different to the national prediction, but the local forecasters should know best for their own area. Meteorologists now admit that one in five forecasts are wrong, so you have an 80 per cent chance of it being correct. Get as good a forecast as you can as close to your time of departure as possible. Telephone or fax forecasts are usually updated around 6am and provide the most up-to-date service available to the general public.

Rocky crags in the Duddon Valley near Seathwaite

Family cycling

Traffic-free cycling on good surfaces is the key to enjoyable family cycling. The easy and some of the medium rides in Chapter 3 are suitable for families. In addition the following areas are of interest. Details of facilities and the appropriate Ordnance Survey Landranger map (or alternative) are included where appropriate.

Forestry Commission holdings and country parks

Miterdale (OS Outdoor Leisure 6) A mixture of mature conifers and native broadleaves. Car parking beside the River Mite.

Broughton Moor (OS Outdoor Leisure 6) Rugged forest, dramatic scenery. Car parking on road between Broughton Mills and Torver.

High Stand (OS 86) Mixed forest 9.5 kms (6 miles) southeast of Carlisle. Informal car parks at GR 490480.

Setmurthy Forest (OS 89) 1.6 kms (1 mile) east of Cockermouth.

Dodd Wood (OS Outdoor Leisure 4) North of Keswick. Carpark, cafe, toilets.

Hardknott Forest (OS Outdoor Leisure 6) Carparking at GR 234996.

No through roads alongside lakes or up valleys

In the heart of the Lake District many quiet or dead-end lanes run alongside lakes or up valleys. Distances given are one way, do as much as you want.

Ullswater (OS 90/Outdoor Leisure 5) 9.5 kms (6 miles) from Pooley Bridge to Bannerdale and Boredale.

Haweswater (OS 90/Outdoor Leisure 5) 13 kms (8 miles) Askham through Bampton Grange.

Longsleddale (OS 90 and 97/Outdoor Leisure 7) 13 kms (8 miles) from Burneside.

Kentmere (OS 90 and 97/Outdoor Leisure 7) 8 kms (5 miles) from Staveley.

Coniston Water (OS 96 or 97) 14.5 kms (9 miles) south from Coniston or north from Spark Bridge.

Dunnerdale (OS 96 and 89 /Outdoor Leisure 6) 11 kms (7 miles) between Ulpha, north of Broughton in Furness and Cockley Beck, and the low point between Hardknott and Wrynose Pass.

Wast Water (OS 89/Outdoor Leisure 6) 16 kms (10 miles) northeast from Gosforth to the Wasdale Head Inn.

Lorton Vale and Loweswater (OS 89/Outdoor Leisure 4) 29-km (18-mile) loop south of Cockermouth through Southwaite and Thackthwaite.

Thirlmere (OS Landranger 90 or Outdoor Leisure 4) 8 kms (5 miles) from the Steel End carpark at the southern end of the lake.

Sustrans Sea to Sea (C2C) route

The Sea to Sea Cycle Route is a 225-km (140-mile) route which leaves the west coast at either Whitehaven or Workington and runs through the northern Lake District before snaking amongst the Durham Dales to Sunderland. It uses minor roads and traffic-free cycle paths. Special sections have been designed with family cyclists and novice bikers of all ages in mind and still present a worthy challenge for the more experienced and adventurous rider. Some parts are high and rugged and should only be attempted with suitable clothing after taking heed of the weather forecast.

LEAFLET AVAILABLE FROM: Sustrans, Rockwood House, Barn Hill, Stanley, County Durham DH9 8AN. Tel: 01207 281259

Cumbria Cycle Way

A circular route 415 kms (259 miles) long, which explores parts of the county rarely visited by tourists including the Eden Valley, the Solway Coast, the almost deserted Mallerstang Valley and Sellafield. The route is waymarked in both directions: travelling clockwise will provide the benefit of prevailing westerly winds along the west coast section. The route is divided into seven stages, averaging 60 km (37 miles) for each section, which is a comfortable day's ride for a reasonably fit person.

LEAFLET AVAILABLE by sending £1.50 payable to Cumbria County Council to: County Planning Department, Cumbria County Council, County Offices, Kendal, Cumbria LA9 4RQ.

Trail techniques

Most of the rides in this guide require no special riding skills. However, if you are undertaking the **two hard rides** or perhaps making up your own on some of the higher fells, below are a few points worth bearing in mind in order to maximise your enjoyment and likelihood of safe return and minimise conflict with other users and damage to the environment.

Climbs

You will tire far less quickly if you can stay in the saddle for as long as possible. This means using all your gears: don't struggle in a high gear if you have an easier one. Shift your weight to the nose of the saddle. Most of the tough climbs in the Lake District will involve pushing your bike and others (though none in this book) will even involve you carrying the bike. If you know that you will have to carry for any distance, fit appropriate padding to the frame of the bike to protect your shoulders from bruising.

Flat, easy cycling on the Keswick Railway Path

Descents

Safety is of paramount importance. Ride within your limits, don't be pushed by your peers into going faster than feels safe. When cycling steeply downhill off-road, keep the pedals level, bend at the knee so that your legs act as springs and keep your weight over the back of the bike, if necessary lowering your saddle and hanging your backside over the back wheel. Don't use the front brake by itself, keep your eye on the trail and leave space between you and the person in front. The

possible consequences of going too fast downhill are serious injury to you or your bike, having to carry a bike with a buckled wheel or damaged frame down a mountainside or explaining to a Mountain Rescue team why you needed to call them out.

Kentmere from near the top of Garburn Pass

Environmental awareness

There are few places in Britain where the pressure of recreational demand is as intense as the Lake District. The advent of the mountain bike and its growing presence in the hills in the last ten years is a very new phenomenon and you should be aware that there is occasional resistance to off-road cycling.

Certain bridleways are so popular with walkers that it really doesn't make sense to ride them at their busiest. They include: the bridleways to the top of Skiddaw, Helvellyn, High Street, and from Wasdale Head past Sty Head and Esk Hause to the Langdales. Try to avoid weekends and the busiest holiday times.

It is also better not to use the bridleways when they are boggy in winter or after prolonged rain – riding through these areas, cutting through soft turf and leaving scars behind is not environmentally sound. Think about leaving these tracks for a dry spell in the summer and stick to stone-based tracks in the winter.

Chapter 2: Setting up, setting out and coming home

The Mountain Bike

Mountain Bikes (MTBs) are one of the most common types of bike in use today. Their main attraction is their versatility: they can be used for commuting, gentle family outings, exhilarating technical challenges and expeditions. They cost anything from £150– £3,000. The rides in this guide are suitable for an 'everyday' mountain bike.

1 Tough frames made from high tensile steel tubing – cromoly tubing is good because it is very strong, relatively light and inexpensive.

2 Saddle – there are two types, shown here is a micro-adjusting saddle for finer position adjustment. The clip type is also commonly used. Most saddles are designed for men and can be extremely uncomfortable on the female form. Women are advised to invest in a saddle designed for them.

3 Wide alloy rims are better than steel, they are easier to straighten, lighter, and provide better braking performance in the wet.

4 There are many types of tyres for MTBs – fat tyres with deep treads are good for mixed on and off-road cycling; thinner, shallow tread tyres are better for road riding.

5 Flat handlebars for an upright riding position.

6 Bar ends provide an extra hand position, useful for easier climbing and cruising on the flat.

7 Derailleur gears – fitted on all MTBs and provide 10-24 gears. The average MTB has 15-18 speeds which is sufficient for easy and medium grade rides. A minimum of 21 gears is necessary for tough off-road routes.

8 Gear shifters – there are four types; Shimano Rapidfire, thumb shifters, grip shifters and down type shifters for road bikes. The most common are rapidfire (shown here) and grip shifters.

9 Grips.

10 Indexed gears – mounted on the handlebar for accessible operation, the gear lever provides an audible and tactile click to indicate a gear change. Some bikes have a switch which disables the indexing.

11 Cantilever brakes – more powerful than traditional caliper brakes and essential for stopping quickly.

Sizing up

When buying a new or second-hand bike it is important to get one that is the correct size. Too big or too small and you could end up with numerous aches and strains. Follow the guidelines below and you should end up with a bike that is suited to your height and frame and is enjoyable to ride.

Sizing

There should be 7-10 cms (3-4 inches) between you and the cross bar when standing astride the bike – this is important if you have to jump off quickly.

Heading

SADDLE HEIGHT – adjust the saddle so that your hips don't rock when pedalling. When the ball of the foot is resting on the pedal, at the bottom of the rotation, the knee should be slightly bent.

◀ POSITION – adjust back or forward so that when the knee is flexed at 45 degrees, the knee and pedal axle are in a straight line.

ANGLE – experiment for a comfortable position.

Handlebars

Height – there is no right or wrong height, adjust for a comfortable fit.

◀ Reach – a good guide is to ensure that your back is at 45 degrees when in a natural riding position, but experiment for personal preference.

Sizing children's bikes

Kids love riding bikes. Mountain bikes are perfect because they get them off the streets and out of the way of traffic. There are many different grades of tracks that are suitable for children to ride on with their parents, a number of which are featured in Chapter 3. Good children's mountain bikes that offer the same sort of features as adult bikes are now available.

Sizing a mountain bike for a child is the same as for an adult. It may be tempting to buy a larger size so that it lasts longer but this is not a good idea because a child will have less control over the bike and may lose confidence.

Good-fitting helmets are particularly important for children (*see* pp 30-31, Essential accessories). Deck your child out with a full complement of reflectors (*see* pp 46-47, Safety and emergency).

Essential accessories

Helmet – always wear a helmet, they can limit damage to one of the most vulnerable parts of the body. A good fit is essential, they should be snug and move with the scalp if you wiggle your eyebrows but not tight enough to pinch the sides of your head. A helmet that does not fit will not offer adequate protection.

Make sure a new helmet conforms to one of the following standards: Snell, ANSI, Eu, and BSI.

If you do have an accident, take the helmet back to the shop that sold it to you for checking. Helmets are designed to withstand one crash and damage is not always apparent to the eye.

Children's helmets

A child's head is especially vulnerable. Get children, and reluctant teenagers, into the habit of wearing a helmet from the start.
Remember
- don't buy a helmet for a child to grow into, a good fit is important
- make sure the helmet sits low enough on the head but has little side to side movement
- ensure the strap is adjusted so that the helmet cannot move
- avoid pinching a child's neck in the snap lock buckle, it is painful. Ask them to hold their chin up
- buy a helmet with some reflective material on the outer shell

Not essential but fun

A bike computer: they are useful for seeing how far you have gone and can tell you your maximum speed, average speed, total accumulated mileage and the time. Most have seven functions and are waterproof.

Tool kit 4, 5, and 6mm allen keys, multi tool (a selection of tools in a penknife format), small pliers, chain rivet extractor, chain ring bolt, spare chain links.

Puncture repair kit

Spare inner tube

Pump

Lights necessary even if you don't expect to be riding in the dusk or dark. You may get delayed. LED lights are compact, light and have a 3-4 month battery life.

Reflective belt in case you run out of daylight or the weather changes dramatically.

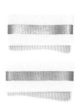

Map this guide uses Ordnance Survey Landranger 1:50,000. You are advised to buy the relevant map(s) for your route and not rely on the maps reproduced in this guide.

Compass

Oil in a small tin or grease in a packet.

Water bottle they vary in size from 0.75 litres to 1.5 litres.

Money and small change or a phone card for emergencies.

A watch to ensure you start the return journey in good time.

Bumbag for carrying money and valuables.

Panniers for carrying food and spare clothing.

Clothing for all weathers

There is a lot of specialist cycling gear in bike shops and the range can be rather daunting to an occasional or novice cyclist. Most people cannot go out and buy the complete outfit in one go and will have to make do with what is in the wardrobe with perhaps one or two specialist items. Here are some general guidelines to cope with the vagaries of the British weather and help make your ride as comfortable as possible.

- Wear loose clothing that allows complete freedom of movement.
- Choose materials such as cotton or Lycra mixes which can breathe.
- If you buy one item of cycling gear, make it a pair of padded cycling shorts, they provide comfort from the saddle and are designed not to chafe the skin.

Being properly dressed for bad weather and good (below) makes riding enjoyable

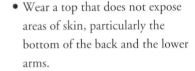

- Wear a top that does not expose areas of skin, particularly the bottom of the back and the lower arms.
- Wear, or pack, several layers of clothing so that you can shed or add as the temperature changes.
- Make sure the layer closest to your skin is made of a material that can breathe.
- Always take a waterproof; cycling in cold wet clothes is miserable.
- Use glasses to protect your eyes from dust, insects and bright sunshine. Specialist cycling glasses (above right) are designed for that purpose.
- Gloves can stop you shredding your hands if you come off the bike and padded ones provide some shock absorption.
  - It is not essential to buy cycling shoes, although if you intend to cycle very regularly it might be a good idea. Tennis shoes and trainers are good substitutes.

Fine weather essentials

- sunglasses
- sun cream
- long sleeved top in case it gets chilly

specialist glasses protect the eyes and are less likely to break

A long sleeved top for riding off-road.

Foul weather essentials

- hat
- scarf
- thermal top and bottom
- several long-sleeved tops for layering
- waterproof boots
- waterproof gloves
- A thermal layer next to the skin in wet or cold conditions maintains core warmth (chest and back)
- A balaclava keeps head and ears warm when it is cold
- Two pairs of gloves and socks keep extremities from getting icy in winter

Wash padded cycling shorts after every ride to keep them in good condition

Tips

- Legs and arms can get scratched when riding off-road, long sleeves and trousers may be more appropriate
- Keep spare clothes in the car – muddy clothes do not mix well with the insides of pubs and tearooms
- Keep a black bin liner in the car for wet and muddy clothes

padded gloves

Food and drink

Your body uses a lot of energy when cycling, particularly on tougher rides, so it is very important to carry food and drink with you, even on the shortest rides. If you rely on the pub or teashop they will inevitably be closed. And if you get delayed by a mechanical fault or an injury, it could be some time before you get to the next watering hole.

The golden rules are to eat before you are hungry and drink before you are thirsty. It is a good idea to find some shelter when you stop for refreshment to avoid getting chilled, particularly in exposed areas of the country. A hollow in the ground will do.

Please remember to take all litter with you when you have finished your snack. Litter can be a major hazard to wildlife and spoils the countryside for other people.

Flapjacks are a favourite mountain biker's snack

Remember to eat before you are hungry

Food

Snacking is better than having one big meal. Complex carbohydrates are the best energy givers. They take longer to digest and release their nutrients at a steady rate. Chocolate and sweet snacks give an immediate energy boost which fades rapidly. Flapjacks, malt loaf, dried fruit, nuts and bananas are all nutritious and easy to carry. Specialist cycling food is sometimes overhyped and overpriced but may be worth a try.

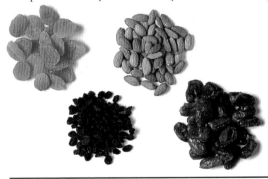

Complex carbohydrates such as bananas, dried fruit and nuts provide energy while you are on the trail

Drink

Water is by far the best drink to carry with you because it is easily absorbed by the body. Dehydration can happen quickly, particularly on long rides in hot weather, therefore aim to drink every 20-30 minutes. Don't underestimate how much water your body can lose on a hard trip, even in winter. Carry some extra water in the car. Don't drink from a stream unless you are sure it is close to a good spring. Avoid sweet and fizzy drinks.

Tip

Clear water bottles help you see if the bottle has gone mouldy and tell you how much is in there.

Preparing your bike

Before you start out on a journey it is good to get into the habit of a pre-ride check. If you are not confident about doing it yourself, many shops will oblige for a small fee. However, the steps below are fairly easy to accomplish and give you the best chance of a trouble-free ride.

1 ► Ensure that all the bolts on the bike are tight.

2 Run through the gears and ensure that the changes are crisp.

3 Look for damaged or stiff links in the chain: spinning the cranks backwards should show you if there is a problem because the chain will jump.

4 Check there is enough lubrication on the chain.

5 Pull on the brake lever, if it moves easily a long way towards the handlebar, the brakes need adjusting.

6 Worn brake blocks will not do their job. Replace them when it becomes necessary.

7 All the strands on a cable should be twisted together. Frayed or rusty brake cable must be replaced immediately.

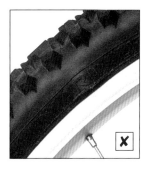

8 Inspect tyres for flints and thorns, gouges from brake blocks and general wear. Worn or damaged tyres are more prone to puncture.

9 Measure the tyre pressure with a pressure gauge. You will find the recommended pressure marked on the sides of the tyre.

If you don't have a gauge, squeeze the tyre sides: you should be able to push your thumb about a ½ cm (¼ inch) into a correctly inflated mountain bike tyre.

Ensure tyres are well inflated for off-road surfaces where punctures are more likely.

10 ▶ Spin the wheels to check if they are straight, using the brake blocks as a guide. Listen for scuffing noises which indicate a dent. Small dents can be hammered out with a rubber mallet, larger ones mean the wheels need replacing.

11 Look for bent and damaged spokes.

Transporting your bike

A lot of people live in cities and cities tend to be a long way from areas where people want to ride their mountain bikes. It is possible to get to the start of some of the routes in this book by train. However, the most usual method of transporting your bike is on, in or behind the car.

By car

Roof racks, boot racks and tow bar racks are the alternatives to bagging (see box) when transporting your bike by car, although just removing the wheels and saddle may be enough to fit a small bike or bikes

into a large car. Secure fixing and regular checking is of the utmost importance whichever of the options you choose.

Tow bar racks are secure and won't damage the car's paint work.

Be legal

Boot and tow bar racks cover up your rear tail lights and number plate. You must use a tow plate with your number plate attached so that other road users can clearly see your brakes and number plate. Many police forces are vigilant about this and may take action if you are in breach of the law.

Bagging your bike

Dismantling your bike and carrying it in a bag is a good way of getting round reluctant train and coach operators and also transporting your bike inside your car. It is important to pad the tubing and wheel to prevent scratches and knocks. It is also essential to double check that you have put all the components into the bag along with the tools needed for reassembly at your destination.

Boot and roof racks

Boot racks are becoming one of the most popular ways of transporting bikes. Up to 99 per cent of cars can be fitted with a boot rack: they are easy to attach and relatively cheap. Most are designed to carry up to three bikes. Roof rack manufacturers offer fitting kits to allow you to carry anything from skis to canoes, including bikes. They can be carried upside down, upright and with the front wheel removed. See the box opposite to ensure you are travelling legally.

Tow bar racks

These can save damage to the body work of your car and are as strong and secure as a boot rack.

By train

Most rail networks will let you take your bike onto their trains. However, policy varies from region to region and country to country so always check before arriving at the station.

By coach and bus

Coach and bus companies have their own policies on transporting bikes, so check in advance that you will be allowed on.

By air

Most major airlines will carry your bike. Check with the airline when you book your tickets. Your bike will have to be boxed up or bagged (*see* above).

Preparing yourself: stretching

Cycling is good exercise and an excellent way of keeping in shape. Like all forms of exercise, you are far less likely to get an injury if you make sure your muscles are warmed up before you start. Simple stretches will greatly improve your flexibility and endurance. The following steps should take 5-10 minutes.

Back

Sit on the floor with your legs stretched out in front of you. Bend your body forwards from the waist/hip aiming to put your nose on your knees. It doesn't matter if you can bend just a couple of inches or all the way. Stop as soon as it hurts.

Legs

Your legs are going to work hardest of all, particularly on a long ride with several climbs. These three exercises will prepare you for what is to come.

◀ Stretch the calf muscles by extending one leg straight behind you, foot flat on the floor, and holding the stretch for 30 seconds. Move your rear foot further back and hold this for 30 seconds. Repeat with the other leg.

Shoulder

Clasp your hands together behind you by reaching your left hand over your shoulder so that your right elbow is pointing straight up and your left hand up behind the back. Hold the position for 30 seconds. Repeat, reversing the position of the arms.

Neck

Stand relaxed and turn your head from left to right slowly, holding it for at least 30 seconds at the farthest reach each side. Then gently raise and lower your chin.

Groin

Sit on the floor with your legs apart at 45 degrees or as far as they will go. With both hands, reach towards the right foot and hold the position for 30 seconds. Repeat to the left.

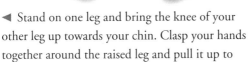

◄ Stand on one leg and bring the knee of your other leg up towards your chin. Clasp your hands together around the raised leg and pull it up to your chest, keeping your back straight. Hold the position for 30 seconds. Repeat with the other leg.

▶ To stretch the hamstring, cross one leg in front of the other, keeping your feet close together. Gently bend forwards as far as you can go from the waist/hip, keeping your back straight. Hold this position for 30 seconds. Repeat, crossing the other leg in front.

On the trail

When out riding, remember that there are other people using the trails for their own enjoyment. Polite, helpful and considerate conduct is important so that mountain bikers are not seen as a menace by the rest of the population. Following the MTB code below will make you a good ambassador for all mountain bikers.

MTB code

1 Give way to other trail users.
2 Always be courteous to other trail users.
3 Take every bit of rubbish away with you.
4 Leave gates as you find them.
5 Never skid, especially on wet soft ground (to avoid erosion).
6 Ride with respect for your surroundings.
7 Check that you have legal access to the land you are on.
8 Always take note of MOD flagpoles.
9 Warn horses and walkers of your approach by ringing your bell, singing, whistling or talking to your cycle partners.

Courtesy to other trail users costs nothing and enhances the reputation of mountain biking

Below are a few tips to make your life easier and safer out on the trail.

- Plan your ride with the weakest member of your group in mind.
- Let the slowest rider set the pace.
- Off-road, leave a reasonable distance between you and the rider in front.
- The deepest part of a puddle is where vehicle wheels go; try the middle higher ground.
- Anticipate hills; change to the right gear in good time.
- On-road, help weaker riders by getting them to ride in your slipstream.
- Remove vegetation from derailleurs (gears) immediately to prevent against damage.
- Faster riders should go ahead and open and close gates for the rest of the group to balance the differences in strength.
- Keep money and keys with you at all times, even if you leave other gear on the bike.
- Fold your map to the section you need in the dry and out of the wind.

Mountain bikers have to share many trails with other users

Navigation

It is easy to get lost while mountain biking. A combination of tight twisty trails and changing scenery makes it easy to become disorientated and lose your sense of direction. Routes also look different according to the time of year.

A LWAYS CARRY a map of the area. You will find the number and name of the map for each ride in this guide in the ride specification box. Observation is the key to successful navigation in unknown territory. Make a mental note of distinctive features such as steep contours, rivers, forested areas and tracks before you begin and look for them on route.

If you become lost, stay in a group and work together to find your way home. Don't separate; both parties may end up lost! Retrace your steps to a point where you know where you are. If necessary go back to the start the way you came. Try to rejoin the route at a later stage or find a road alternative on the map. If you can't do this, stop at the next signpost or landmark, consult your map and take a compass bearing.

Checking the map to decide in which direction to continue

Taking a compass bearing

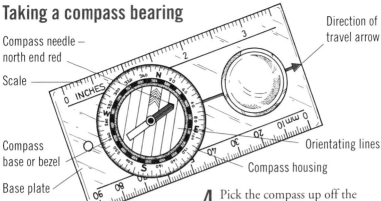

Compass needle – north end red

Scale

Direction of travel arrow

Compass base or bezel

Base plate

Orientating lines

Compass housing

A compass becomes essential once you are lost and is always useful in forestry areas. The illustration above shows the most useful type of compass which usually comes with instructions. The following steps will help you determine in which direction to travel according to the route on your map.

1 Roughly orientate the map so the north edge is facing north.

2 Place the compass flat on the map with the long edge of the baseplate along the desired direction of travel. In other words either connecting, or in line with, where you are currently standing and the next point on the route.

3 Rotate the capsule until the N on the compass dial or bezel, not the needle, points to North on the map. You have now taken a bearing.

4 Pick the compass up off the map and turn yourself around until the red end of the needle points to N on the compass dial and lines up with the orientating lines in the base of the dial. The large 'direction of travel' arrow will now point precisely at your destination.

5 Choose a landmark on this line of travel and ride towards it without looking at the compass: there is no need and minor curves and deviations in the track will only confuse the issue.

6 When you reach this first landmark repeat the procedure until you reach your destination.

Safety and emergency

Safety is, of course, a priority – particularly if you are riding with children. There is a lot that common sense will tell you. However, a few reminders are always useful.

Safety precautions

- Always wear a helmet, even on the shortest route. You can never predict what other track and road users are going to do. The one time you go out without your helmet on is the time you will most need it. Nothing can prevent the damage that a car speeding at 60mph causes, but protecting your head can limit injury in lot of instances.

- Take great care crossing roads, particularly main A roads. Dismount, and use a pedestrian crossing if there is one. Read ahead in the ride directions to alert yourself to road crossings and warn others in your group, especially children, that a road is coming up.

- Avoid riding on busy roads with young children and inexperienced riders. Try to find a quieter alternative.

- If you are riding in poor light or at night, make sure your lights are on and that you are wearing some reflective clothing. Ankle bands are particularly good at alerting car drivers to your presence. Also, kit your children out with the full range of reflectors.

- Check the local weather forecast before you embark on a ride, particularly if you intend to be out for a long time. Try to make a educated guess as to whether it is riding weather.

- Tell someone where you are going and, if possible, leave a marked up map of the area at home. It will help locate you in the event of a rescue team being called out.

- Take adequate supplies of food and drink to prevent against dehydration. Don't be over ambitious. Choose a ride well within your capabilities or you might find yourself in trouble in the middle of a route.

What to do in emergencies

Due to the nature of off-road riding it is quite possible that you may have to deal with an accident involving another rider. There are several things to remember:

- Place the rider in the recovery position using the minimum of movement (see First aid pp48-49). Keep the rider warm and place a jacket underneath their head for comfort
- If they have sustained a head injury do not remove their helmet unless they are bleeding severely
- Do not give food in case they need to be operated on in a hurry
- If you have to leave an injured rider to seek assistance make sure that they are warm and feel able to stay awake
- Make a note of where you have left them on your map and mark the spot with a piece of bright clothing held down by a stone or attached to a tree
- Get help as quickly as possible

Keep an accident victim warm and get help as soon as possible

First Aid

Every mountain biker, indeed every cyclist, comes off their bike sooner or later. It is a good idea to carry a small first aid kit with you on trips to cope with cut and bruises.

When a person is seriously injured the priority is to ring 999 and get an ambulance to them as quickly as possible. Describe your location as accurately as you can. It is useful to be able to tell the emergency services as much as possible about the accident and the state of the patient when they arrive.

Minor injuries

- Small cuts and grazes can be rinsed with cold water from a drinking bottle. Apply some antiseptic and cover with a clean plaster.

- Dizziness and faintness might occur after a crash or spill. Sit down comfortably until the feeling passes. If it doesn't improve place the head between the knees.

Simple first aid kit

- As a minimum, take the following: water bottle, antiseptic lotion or cream, plasters, cottonwool.

Major injuries

- If someone has a serious crash or spill remaining calm is vital. You cannot help another person if you are in a panic. Don't expect too much of yourself: you may be suffering from shock as well as the injured party.

- Assess the situation. Stop the traffic if it may be a danger to the injured person and try to enlist the help of a third party.

- Assess the injured. Are they conscious? If they are, ask them how they feel and if they can describe their injuries.

- Bleeding needs to be stopped. If possible raise the wound and apply a compress firmly over the bleeding area until it ceases.

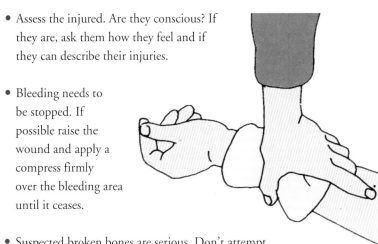

- Suspected broken bones are serious. Don't attempt to move the victim unless absolutely necessary until professional help arrives.

- Check for a pulse by placing your fingers on the victim's voice box. If there is no pulse and their breathing has stopped you could try resuscitation – however, only do so if you know how.

- Keep the injured person warm, offer reassuring words and hold their hand until help arrives. Don't give them food or drink in case they need an emergency operation.

- If you are sure the injured person does not have a spinal injury, place them in the recovery position.

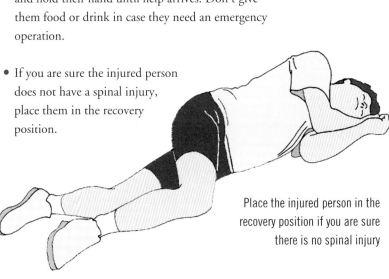

Place the injured person in the recovery position if you are sure there is no spinal injury

When you get home

Cleaning the bike after a ride is a job most people hate and would skip if they had any choice. However, it is essential if you want to maximise the life of your bike and ensure it is always in good working order. The following is a six step procedure which should take about 10 minutes.

Tools

Ideally use a hose with a brush head and soap reservoir, car shampoo and WD40 for lubrication. Keep high pressure water spraying away from the bearings in case the seals cannot withstand a strong jet of water.

1 Hose off the worst of the mud while it is still wet.

2 Use a hose brush head (or a brush and hose) to scrub off any lumps of mud and finish the initial rinse.

3 Using car shampoo, gently scrub off remaining dirt with soapy water.

4 Rinse off the soap with plain water and repeat the shampoo and rinse if necessary.

5 Use degreaser on ground-in dirt and rinse off with plain water.

6 Let the water drip off and spray exposed metal or moving parts with WD40.

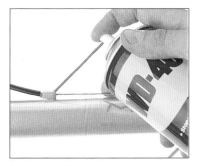 

Lubrication

WD40 is an adequate and relatively cheap oil for general lubrication. Apply it immediately after cleaning to:

1 rear brake pivots
2 rear mech pivot points
3 rear mech jockey wheels
4 front mech points

5 brake lever pivots
6 front brake pivots
7 cable ends at the stops

Use a heavier oil such as standard mineral-based medium weight oil for the chain.

Chapter 3: The Rides

1 Whitehaven to Rowrah

The Whitehaven to Rowrah railway path is the flagship of West Cumbria Groundwork Trust who have embarked on a far-reaching and imaginative project to create recreational trails on the west coast of Cumbria. Complete with trailside sculptures, the paths have gentle gradients and are an excellent facility for all the family.

GRADE easy

DISTANCE up to 30 kms (18.6 miles). Can be linked to ride no. 2 Ennerdale Water

TIME allow 3.5 hours for full length trip

MAP OS Landranger 89 West Cumbria

GRID REFERENCE AT START Whitehaven 971182 Cleator Moor 018152 Rowrah 057185

PARKING Whitehaven: by the recreation ground/football club; Cleator Moor: around the main square; Rowrah, just off the A5086 west of Station Inn

TRAINS nearest station, Whitehaven

TERRAIN urban roads, old mining and quarrying areas, farmland

SEASONAL SUITABILITY all year

SURFACE tarmac or consolidated aggregates

CLIMBS/DESCENTS ride is one long steady climb

REFRESHMENTS full facilities in Whitehaven and Cleator Moor; pubs in Frizington and Rowrah

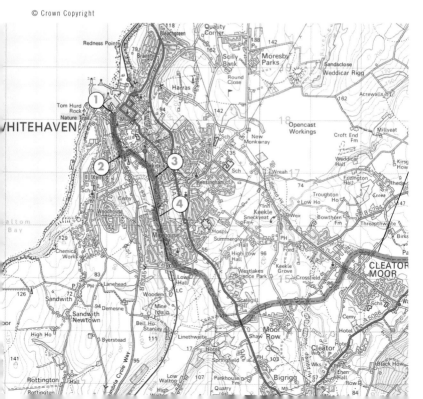

Whitehaven harbour

1 Start at the harbour/Royal Standard PH in Whitehaven, cross the main road via the pelican crossing, go past the Vine PH then turn right along Market Place, King Street and James Street. At the T-junction at the end of James Street, opposite the YMCA, turn right, then left.

2 Go past some supermarkets. Soon after passing the Punch Bowl PH on the left, turn left signposted 'Barrow (A5094)'. After 90 m (100 yds) at the bottom of a gentle hill, ignore the first right to the recreation ground and football club. Take the second right just before a railway crossing. (From here onwards the route is shielded from traffic.)

D irection 1 and the first half of 2 take you along busy town centre roads. Starting from the recreation ground carpark in Whitehaven, the route is almost traffic-free. Cleator Moor is a better starting place for kids.

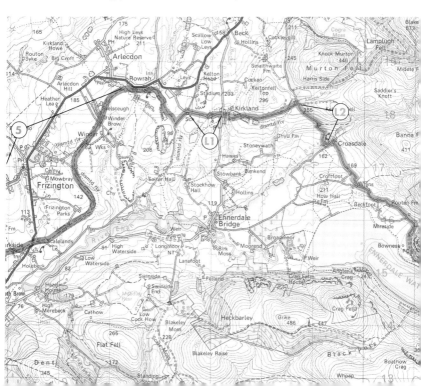

3 Follow the track under a railway bridge. At the T-junction opposite Pow Avenue, turn right. As the road swings left uphill, by a modern primary school, bear right then left onto a tarmac track. You should soon start finding 'C2C' and railway path signposts.

4 Follow the signposts underneath, then parallel to, the railway. At the T-junction with the road by some houses bear left (straight ahead) then after 50 m (55 yds), by a waymark, turn left onto a parallel, house-lined street. After 90 m (100 yds) turn left again to join the trail proper.

5 Follow the trail to Cleator Moor, 6.5 kms (4 miles) from the start, and Rowrah 8 kms (5 miles) from the start.

✚ Link 1 To link with Ennerdale Water (ride no 2) follow railway path signs for 1.6 kms (1 mile) beyond Rowrah until the path ends at a carved twisted wooden arch. Turn left onto the road, then at the crossroads by Lamplugh School turn right. At the next crossroads in Kirkland go straight ahead signposted 'Croasdale'. Continue for 2 kms (3.2 miles).

✚ Link 2 At the T-junction at the top of the hill turn right. At the T-junction at the bottom of a steep hill turn left signposted 'Roughton, Ennerdale Water' to join the road/track alongside the lake. Continue for 2.4 kms (1.5 miles) past the llamas at Routen Farm to the start of the lakeside trail.

2 Ennerdale Water

One of four rides in this guide which uses Forestry Commission land, the route along the steeply wooded hills above atmospheric Ennerdale Water and the Valley of the River Lisa takes you right into the heart of the central fells. A link to ride no. 1, Whitehaven to Rowrah, takes you past a llama farm at Routen Farm and to Keltonfell Top where you can see across to Wales and Scotland.

GRADE easy	
DISTANCE 18 kms (11 miles) with a link to ride no 1, Whitehaven to Rowrah	
TIME allow 2 hours	
MAP OS Landranger 89 West Cumbria/Outdoor Leisure 4 (Lakes North West)	
GRID REF AT START 110152	
PARKING carpark on northern edge of Ennerdale Water, from the A5086 nr Cleator Moor follow signs for Ennerdale and the forest	
TERRAIN forestry land and fells	
SEASONAL SUITABILITY all year	
SURFACE good quality forestry tracks	
CLIMBS/DESCENTS 1 main climb/1 main descent	
REFRESHMENTS none on route	

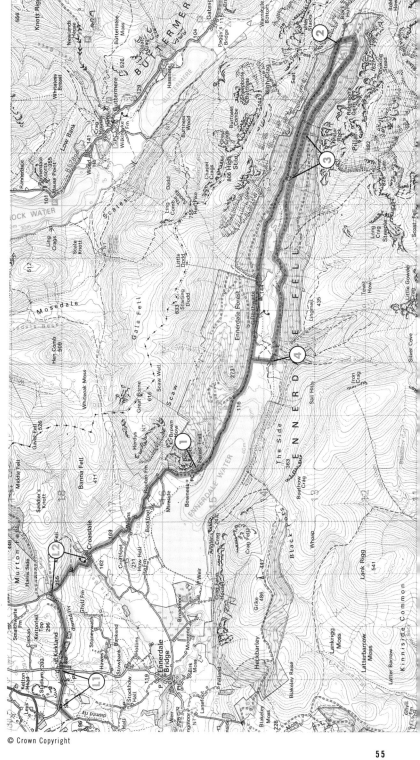

55

Looking towards Great Gable

1 Start at the carpark at the northern edge of Ennerdale Water. Turn left up the valley and follow the track for 8.8 kms (5.5 miles), staying on the left-hand side of the river, aiming for the bulk of Green Gable and Great Gable.

2 At a bridlegate and a sign for Black Sail Youth Hostel, bear right downhill to cross the River Liza and return along its south side. Continue for 2 kms (1.25 miles).

3 At the first fork after the bridge, bear right. Continue for 1.2 kms (0.75 miles). At the second fork, by a bridge over the river, bear left slightly uphill. Continue for 3.5 kms (2.2 miles) on the broad forestry track on the south side of the valley, climbing occasionally.

4 Follow the obvious main track as it swings right, through a gate and over the river. At the T-junction turn left to return to the start.

✚ Link 2 To link with ride no 1, Whitehaven to Rowrah, go past the carpark away from the forest and lake for 2.4 kms (1.5 miles), passing the llamas at Routen Farm. Take the first road right, just past a telephone box, signposted 'Lamplugh'. At the top of a steep hill take the first road left signposted 'Kirkland, Rowrah'.

✚ Link 1 At the crossroads in Kirkland go straight ahead signposted 'Frizington, Egremont'. Take the first road left at the crossroads by Lamplugh School then the first track right through a carved, twisted wooden arch, this is easily missed. The railway path can be followed for 14.5 kms (9 miles) through Cleator Moor to Whitehaven.

High Beck tumbling from Pillar

3 Grizedale Forest

Grizedale Forest is a Forestry Commission showpiece. Miles of waymarked cycle trails, and many more which are unmarked, provide a wealth of opportunities. The broad forest tracks undulate through the woodland with occasional clearings offering fine views towards Fairfield. This ride could be linked to ride no. 6, Claife Heights and Lake Windermere. Take care not to stray onto footpaths or waymarked walks.

GRADE easy

DISTANCE 10.5 kms (6.5 miles)

TIME allow 1.5 hours/2 hours

MAP OS Landranger 96 or 97/Outdoor Leisure 7 (SE Lakes). Best guide is the Forestry Commission Guide Map available from Grizedale Forest Visitor Centre

GRID REF AT START 335944

PARKING Grizedale Forest Visitor Centre (pay and display); from Hawkshead follow signs for the ferry, then pick up signs for Grizedale; from Newby Bridge follow the A590 to Haverthwaite and turn right at the crossroads for Grizedale

TRAINS/FERRY nearest station, Windermere. From Windermere catch the ferry from Bowness to Sawrey

TERRAIN rolling forestry with clearings

SEASONAL SUITABILITY all year

SURFACE top quality forestry tracks

CLIMBS/DESCENTS 2 good climbs/1 gentle descent

REFRESHMENTS snack bar/restaurant at Grizedale Visitor Centre; Eagles Head PH, Satterthwaite

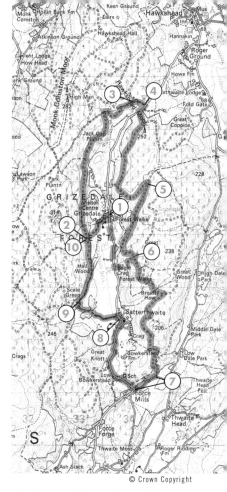

© Crown Copyright

1 Start at Grizedale Forest Visitor Centre carpark. Turn right out of the carpark. Immediately after the Forestry Enterprise offices, turn right onto the tarmac lane signposted 'Bike Route. Moor Top 2.8 miles, High Cross 5.2 miles'. As the road swings sharp right, bear left over the cattle grid onto a blue cycle route.

2 Climb steadily for 300 m (330 yds). Go through the bridlegate by a second cattle grid and turn sharply right uphill still on the blue bike route.

Rhododendrons on the northern edge of Grizedale Forest

3 At a fork of tracks, with red and blue markers, bear right following the blue route.

4 At the T-junction with the road by Moor Top carpark turn right. Ignore the first track to the left signposted 'Footpath to High Barn'. After 100 m (110 yds) take the next track left uphill signposted 'Bike route Bogle Crag 3 miles. Blind Lane 5.8 miles'.

5 Follow the white cycle route signs for 1.6 kms (1 mile). At the T-junction by a post with number 1 on it turn sharp right keeping to the white cycle route. There follows a long descent over 1.6 kms (1 mile) then a short climb passing a small rock face to the left.

6 At a T-junction with yellow and white bike markers:
For the short route, bear right downhill then at the T-junction with the road by Bogle Crag carpark turn right to return to the start;
For the long route turn left sharply uphill and go to direction no. 7.

7 Follow the yellow cycle route, climb up and downhill. At the T-junction with a road turn right uphill. At the next T-junction turn right signposted 'Satterthwaite 1, Grizedale 2'.

8 Go past the church in Satterthwaite. Towards the end of the village, opposite a house called Bracken Ghyll, take the first track left signposted 'Bridleway to Coniston'.

9 Climb the hill, go through the gate adjacent to bridlegate. At a T-junction of forestry tracks turn right.

10 After almost 1.6 kms (1 mile) at a fork of tracks, bear right downhill on the blue cycle route to return to the start.

4 Keswick Railway Path

Running through the beautiful wooded valley of the River Greta, this converted dismantled railway provides an excellent escape route from Keswick avoiding the horrendously busy A66. It also links Keswick with various possibilities from Threlkeld.

1 From the Leisure Pool carpark in Keswick, go past the platform of the old station.

2 There is a short steep climb under the new road bridge where the A66 crosses the River Greta, followed by a narrow section with steps. Show particular consideration to other railway path users here.

3 The path ends after 5.5 kms (3.5 miles) at the A66 just before the village of Threlkeld. In Threlkeld choose between: returning to the start; linking with the Keswick Coach Road ride, no. 5; return to Keswick via lanes and Castlerigg Stone Circle, south of the A66; or follow the B5322 south from Threlkeld through St John's in the Vale to explore Thirlmere; or stop in Threlkeld for refreshment.

GRADE	easy
DISTANCE	11.5 kms (7 miles) with a link to ride no 5, Keswick Coach Road
TIME	allow 1.5 hours
MAP	OS Landranger 90/Outdoor Leisure 4 North West Lakes
GRID REF AT START	273237
PARKING	Leisure pool, northwest side of Keswick
TERRAIN	wooded river valley
SEASONAL SUITABILITY	all year
SURFACE	consolidated stone track
CLIMBS/DESCENTS	steps beneath the main A66 bridge
REFRESHMENTS	full facilities in Keswick; Horse and Farrier PH, Salutation Inn, Threlkeld

A crossing over the River Greta

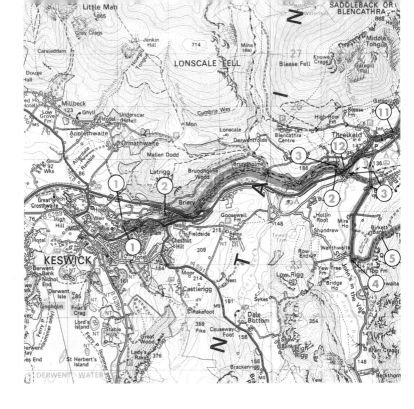

5 Keswick Coach Road

The mountain of Blencathra dominates this ride which climbs to over 420 m (1400 ft) as it runs beneath Clough Head and Wolf Crags.

GRADE medium/hard	
DISTANCE 36 kms (22.5 miles)	
TIME allow 4 hours	
MAP OS Landranger 90 Penrith & Keswick	
GRID REF AT START 273237	
PARKING leisure pool, northwest side of Keswick	
TERRAIN wooded river valley, farmland, pasture, old coachroad over fell	
SEASONAL SUITABILITY all year	
SURFACE mainly tarmac, short rough/muddy section	
CLIMBS/DESCENTS 1 long climb	
REFRESHMENTS Troutbeck Inn, junction of A5091 and A66	

1 From the leisure pool carpark in Keswick, go past the platform of the old station. Follow the railway path for 5.5 kms (3.5 miles). There is a short steep climb under the new road bridge where the A66 crosses the River Greta, followed by a narrow section with steps. Show particular consideration to other railway path users here.

2 Near the end of the railway path, do not cross the final bridge over

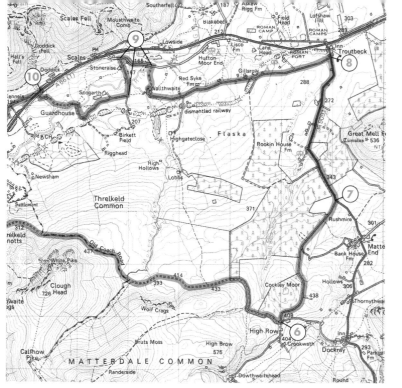

© Crown Copyright

Blencathra from near Guardhouse

the river – the bridlegate bears the sign 'A66 Threlkeld village' – but bear right, away from the railway path, through another bridlegate. Pass beneath the road bridge and leave the railway path opposite Newbridge Cottage.

3 Turn left, then after 100 m (110 yds) just before a road sign for the A66 ahead, turn right through a bridlegate onto a continuation of the railway path. Descend to the B5322 and turn right. Follow for 1.6 kms (1 mile).

4 Shortly after passing a turning to the right signposted 'Keswick and the Church of St John's in the Vale' take the next left signposted 'Matterdale, unsuitable for motors, C2C cycle route'.

5 At a diagonally offset crossroads go straight ahead. Follow the old coach road for 8 kms (5 miles) climbing to 440m (1450ft)

6 Turn left at the T-junction with the road signposted 'Troutbeck'. Continue for 3.2 kms (2 miles).

7 At the T-junction with the A5091 turn left downhill for 3.2 kms (2 miles).

8 180 m (200 yds) before the A66 take the first road left signposted 'Caravan, camp site'. Continue for 5 kms (3 miles).

9 At the T-junction immediately after a cattle grid turn left. Climb the hill and take the first road left at a triangle of grass. At a sign for 'No through road'

follow the road round to the right. Continue for 2.5 kms (1.5 miles).

10 Turn left at the T-junction, take extreme care on the busy A66. Ignore the first track to the right through a field gate and keep an eye out for a narrow track climbing between trees 50 m (55 yds) further on. This is easily missed.

11 At the T-junction at the edge of Threlkeld turn right.

12 Go through Threlkeld, past the village inns, just before the A66 by a 'Give Way in 50 yards' signpost, turn right onto path signposted 'Keswick Railway Path'. Follow the railway path back to the start.

6 Claife Heights and Lake Windermere

Across the water from the popular and often crowded Windermere is the densely wooded west side and a lakeside track which provides some of the easiest cycling in the Lake District. The full loop involves a 180m (600ft) climb through forestry, views of the fells to the north and three delightful tarns.

GRADE easy/medium

DISTANCE 11 kms (7 miles)/13 kms (8 miles).

TIME allow 1.5 hours/2 hours

MAP OS Landranger 90 Penrith & Keswick and 97 Kendal to Morecambe/Outdoor Leisure 7 South East Lakes

GRID REF AT START 398959

PARKING Slipway carpark at the ferry, Lake Windermere

TRAINS/FERRY nearest station, Windermere; ferry from Bowness every 15 minutes all day, all year

TERRAIN lakeside track, forestry, open country

SEASONAL SUITABILITY all year except between directions no. 8-10.

SURFACE tarmac, good lakeside track, good forestry tracks, slightly muddy/rough section

CLIMBS/DESCENTS 1 main climb/1 main descent

REFRESHMENTS pubs, Far Sawrey and ferry terminal; full facilities, Hawkshead

1 From the ferry take the B5285 towards Hawkshead for 0.8 kms (0.5 miles). Then on a sharp left-hand bend, turn first right.

2 The tarmac turns to track and continues alongside the lake for almost 5 kms (3 miles). Where the tarmac restarts, immediately after stone pillars and gates, bear right onto a broad gravel track into Red Nab carpark (National Trust sign). Continue for 1.2 kms (0.75 miles).

3 At the T-junction with the road by a stone lodge on the left and a sign for St Margaret's Church on the right, turn left. Climb the hill into High Wray.

4 Ignore the first left signposted 'Ferry'. After 90 m (100 yds) take the next left signposted 'Basecamp. Bridleway to Claife Heights'.

5 Climb steeply for 0.8 kms (0.5 miles). Lift your bike over the wooden gate to continue climbing on the broad forestry track. *Or*, as the track swings right before the gate, bear left signposted 'Basecamp' then bear right through the bridlegate to rejoin the main track higher up.

6 At a major fork of tracks bear right onto the upper track.

7 At the top of the climb, at the crossroads of tracks, go straight ahead for Sawrey and the ferry. (To return to Hawkshead from here follow the bridleway and Hawkshead signs to the road, turn left through Colthouse then right at the T-junction with the B5285)

8 (*See* below for an alternative start from/return to Hawkshead.) At the next crossroads of tracks by a four-way signpost, turn right towards 'Bridleway, Sawrey'. After a short, steep push/climb, at the T-junction with a broad forestry track, bear right. Go past three small lakes and down the hill.

9 At a fork of bridleways bear left signposted 'Far Sawrey' and go through the gate.

10 At the T-junction with tarmac bear right. At the T-junction with the B5285 bear left past Sawrey Hotel and follow signs for the ferry to return to the start.

Family cycling on Claife Heights

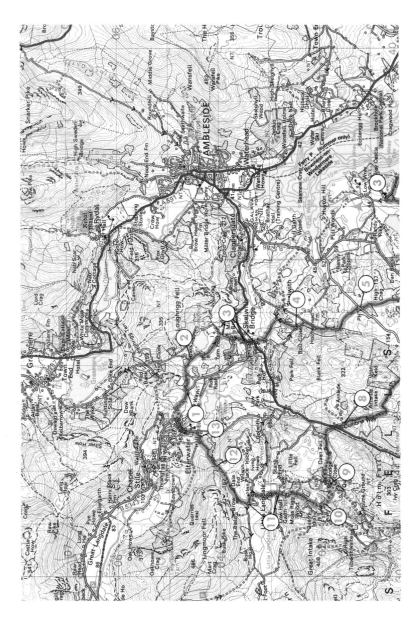

Hawkshead is a good base for several rides. The following three steps allow you to join the route from here.

★ **A1** From Hawkshead, turn right out of the main carpark by the Tourist Information Centre, turn right again signposted 'Windermere via ferry' then at the T-junction turn left signposted 'Sawrey, Windermere'. Immediately after the bridge turn first left signposted 'Wray, Wray Castle'.

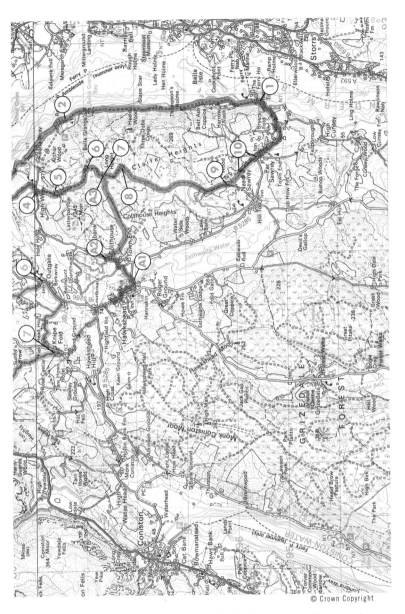

© Crown Copyright

A2 Go through Colthouse and start climbing. Ignore a right turn to the Friends Meeting House. Shortly after passing a lane to the left, and just before Gill Bank, turn sharply right on the next track signposted 'Bridleway, Claife Heights'.

A3 Climb up and over the brow of the hill. At the crossroads of bridleways turn right signposted 'Ferry, Far Sawrey' and join the main route at direction no. 8.

7 Elterwater

Starting at the attractive village of Elterwater this ride takes in a beautiful landscape of wooded hills, steep green fields and drystone walls typical of this part of the country. The section from Knipe Fold to Oxen Fell provides an ever-changing kaleidoscope of Lakeland cameos.

1 From the Post Office in Elterwater take the road signposted 'Ambleside 4'. At the T-junction with the busy B5343 turn right continue for 0.5 kms (0.3 miles) then shortly after crossing the cattle grid take the first left signposted '6ft 6ins width limit'.

2 Ignore a turning to the right. At the T-junction turn right signposted 'Ambleside, Coniston'.

3 Shortly after passing Loughrigg Tarn on the left, take the next road right (no signpost). At the T-junction with the A593 turn right signposted 'Coniston', cross the bridge then turn first left signposted 'Unsuitable for caravans'.

4 Follow signs for Hawkshead. At the T-junction at the top of the hill turn left signposted 'Hawkshead, Coniston via tarns'. Continue for 1 km (0.6 miles).

5 At the crossroads by the Drunken Duck PH go straight ahead signposted 'Hawkshead, Ferry'.

GRADE medium	
DISTANCE 16 kms (10 miles)	
TIME allow 2 hours	
MAP OS Landranger 90 Penrith & Keswick and 97 Kendal to Morecambe/Outdoor Leisure 7 South East Lakes	
GRID REF AT START 329051	
PARKING carpark in Elterwater village and just north of the B5343	
TRAINS nearest station, Windermere	
TERRAIN woodland, farmland, old quarries, low-lying fells	
SEASONAL SUITABILITY all year	
SURFACE tarmac, good quality stone tracks	
CLIMBS/DESCENTS 3 climbs/3 descents	
REFRESHMENTS full facilities, Elterwater; Rosewood Tea Gardens, Skelwith Bridge; Drunken Duck Inn, direction no. 5; Outgate Inn, direction no. 6. Three Shires PH, Langdale	

6 At the T-junction with the B5286, by the Outgate Inn, turn right, continue for 0.8 kms (0.5 miles) then take the first road right signposted 'Field Head, Knipe Fold'.

7 At the T-junction at the top of a short hill bear left, then immediately after a turning to Borwick Lodge on the left and before a left turn to Hawkshead, turn sharply right onto a tarmac drive signposted 'Unsuitable for motors'. This is easily missed. Climb for 2 kms (1.25 miles).

8 At the T-junction with a tarmac track (High Arnside Farm is to your right) bear left downhill. At the crossroads with the A593 go straight ahead signposted 'National Trust, Oxen Fell, Bridleway'.

9 The tarmac turns to track at the High Oxen Fell Farm. Go through a gate and then downhill. At the T-junction with a tarmac track turn left, then opposite a house turn first right onto a gravel track.

10 At a three-way split of tracks by a huge pile of quarry stone on the left, go straight ahead on the middle, sunken track between walls. The rocky surface soon improves. Follow signs for 'Little Langdale'.

11 Cross the bridge – or go through the ford if your bike needs a wash. The track turns to tarmac. At the T-junction by a telephone box turn left, go past the chapel, then first right signposted 'Unsuitable for motor vehicles'.

12 The tarmac turns to track by Dale End Farm. Stay on the main, downhill track, ignoring a bridleway to the left immediately after a gate.

13 At the T-junction with tarmac bear right downhill. At the next T-junction turn left signposted 'Elterwater, Ambleside'. Go past the youth hostel and over the bridge to return to the start.

Along the Cumbria Way north of Knipe Fold

8 Blengdale Forest

Starting at Gosforth, a handsome stone-built village, the third ride through Forestry Commission land takes you on broad stone-based tracks ideal for hybrid and mountain bikes and wide enough to have a conversation when the gradient is relatively gentle.

GRADE medium	
DISTANCE 20 kms (12.5 miles)	
TIME allow 2.5 hours	
MAP OS Landranger 89 West Cumbria/Outdoor Leisure 6 South West Lakes	
GRID REF AT START 067036	
PARKING carpark in Gosforth	
TRAINS nearest station Seascale	
TERRAIN forestry, moorland	
SEASONAL SUITABILITY all year	
SURFACE excellent forestry track	
CLIMBS/DESCENTS 1 long climb/1 long descent	
REFRESHMENTS full facilities, Gosforth	

Worm Gill beneath Lank Rigg

1 Start at the main carpark in Gosforth. Turn left out of the carpark and take the first road left signposted 'Nether Wasdale, Wasdale Head'. Follow for almost 1.6 kms (1 mile).

2 Take the first proper road left by a triangle of grass and a telephone box. After 90 m (100 yds) as the road swings sharp left, bear right (straight ahead) signposted 'Mill House Farm'. Climb steadily for 4 kms (2.5 miles)

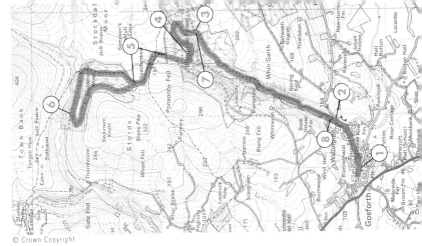

© Crown Copyright

ignoring the left turn by Blengdale House immediately after crossing the river.

3 At a major fork of forestry tracks, bear left downhill to cross the bridge.

4 Over the next mile, climb, descend, then climb again as the track swings right in an arc, southwest, west then north.

5 Leave the forest, go past the remote farm at Scalderskew and enter Scalderskew Wood. Go over a cattle grid at the start of the woodland, then at a fork of tracks bear right gently downhill. The track swings left to follow the valley of the River Calder.

6 The track turns sharply left again just beyond a large vehicle turning area. Follow the track back past Scalderskew Farm, retracing the outward route, following the main track as it descends, climbs then descends to cross the bridge.

7 At the T-junction turn right and follow the track for 4 kms (2.5 miles) as it turns to tarmac near Blengdale House and descends to the road.

8 At the T-junction at the end of the forestry road go straight ahead towards the telephone box. At the T-junction with the more major road bear right. At the next T-junction in Gosforth turn right to return to the start.

A waterfall on the River Bleng

9 Quiet lanes north of Kendal

For a town that is dominated by traffic and the accompanying noise, Kendal is surprisingly close to a network of quiet lanes that carry almost no traffic at all. There are views north to the hills either side of the valleys of the rivers Sprint and Kent. From the turning near the A684 almost all the way back to Burneside, this ride follows quiet lanes rich with wildflowers, past outlying farms, lush fields grazed by sheep and cattle, long miles of drystone walls and glades of deciduous trees. A wonderful exploration of this forgotten corner of Cumbria.

© Crown Copyright

GRADE medium

DISTANCE 24 kms (15 miles)

TIME allow 2.25 hours

MAP OS Landranger 97 Kendal to Morecambe

GRID REF AT START 506956

PARKING Burneside, carpark by bottle banks just beyond Spar shop

TRAINS nearest station, Burneside

TERRAIN woodland, farmland, low lying fells, river valleys

SEASONAL SUITABILITY all year

SURFACE tarmac

CLIMBS/DESCENTS 1 steep climb

REFRESHMENTS Jolly Anglers PH, Burneside

1 With your back to the Jolly Anglers PH in Burneside turn left, then first left signposted 'Skelsmergh (A6), Longsleddale'.

2 Continue for 3 kms (2 miles) this may be busy. At the T-junction with the A6 turn right signposted 'Kendal' then turn first left signposted 'Meal Bank'.

3 At the T-junction turn right over the bridge then immediately left. Keep alongside the river then climb steeply for 1.2 kms (0.75 miles).

4 At the T-junction with the A685 turn right, then left signposted 'Oxenholme'. There follows a steady climb over 3 kms (2 miles).

5 At the crossroads turn left signposted 'Sedbergh'.

6 Just before the A684 turn left. Continue for 1.2 kms (0.75 miles).

7 At the T-junction turn left. Follow this lane under power lines and past a small conifer plantation.

8 At the T-junction immediately after Kiln Head Cottage turn left, then right signposted 'Moorfold, Thatchmoor Head'.

9 At the T-junction bear left and left again (not the gated road).

10 At the T-junction with the A685 in Grayrigg turn left, then right by the church signposted 'Whinfell'. Follow for 3 kms (2 miles).

11 Immediately after crossing the bridge over the River Mint turn right. Go beneath one set of power lines. Just before the second set at the crossroads turn left signposted 'Kendal'.

12 At the T-junction with the A6 turn right then left signposted 'Garth Row'.

13 Cross the bridge over the River Sprint, and climb steeply. At the T-junction, by a 'Footpath to Sprint Bridge' sign, turn left.

14 At the T-junction near Burneside turn right, signposted 'Burneside' to return to the start.

10 Quiet lanes south of Windermere

The scenery here is softer than on the central fells with land devoted to pasture set around whitewashed stone farmhouses and copses of deciduous trees. The ride can easily be linked to ride no. 11, North of Cartmel, to make a 56.5-km (35-mile) cigar-shaped loop.

1 From the Tourist Information Centre in Windermere follow the one way system towards Bowness. 135 m (150 yds) after the end of the one way system turn left by Ellerthwaite Lodge onto Ellerthwaite Road and then first left onto Holly Road. At the crossroads go straight ahead onto Park Road.

2 Follow Park Road past the recreation ground and Heathwaite Post Office. At the brow of the hill turn left onto Lickbarrow Road. Climb steeply and follow this for 2 kms (1.25 miles).

3 At the crossroads with the B5284 go straight ahead signposted 'Winster'. Continue for 1.6 kms (1 mile).

4 At the T-junction with the A5074 turn left, go through Winster, then at the crossroads by the Brown Horse PH turn first right signposted 'Bowland Bridge, Winster Church'. Continue for 5.5 kms (3.5 miles) ignoring turnings to the left and right.

GRADE medium

DISTANCE 28 kms (17.5 miles) with a link to ride no 11, North of Cartmel

TIME allow 2.5 hours

MAP OS Landranger 97 Kendal to Morecambe

GRID REF AT START 413987

PARKING carparks in Windermere (pay and display)

TRAINS nearest station, Windermere

TERRAIN woodland, farmland, low lying fells

SEASONAL SUITABILITY all year

SURFACE tarmac

CLIMBS/DESCENTS 3 climbs

REFRESHMENTS Brown Horse PH, Winster; Hare & Hounds PH, Bowland Bridge; Punch Bowl PH, Crosthwaite; The Sun PH, Crook

5 At the next T-junction turn right, then left by the Hare & Hounds PH signposted 'Witherslack Grange'.

6 Go downhill, cross the bridge, then climb a short steep hill. ✚ Continue straight ahead for 1 km (0.6 miles). At the T-junction by a triangle of grass turn left signposted 'Crosthwaite, Kendal'.

7 At the crossroads with the A5074 go straight ahead signposted 'Unsuitable for HGVs'.

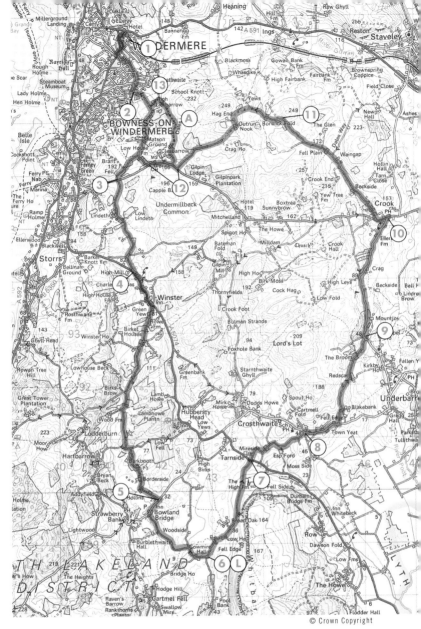
© Crown Copyright

8 At the T-junction with the main road through Crosthwaite turn right. Ignore a left turn by Rose Bank House and after 0.8 kms (0.5 miles) take the next left by a triangle of grass, signposted 'Red Scar, Brown Farm'.

Continue for 1.6 kms (1 mile).

9 Turn left at the T-junction by a triangle of grass. Continue for 3 kms (2 miles) ignoring a left turn after 0.8 kms (0.5 miles).

10 At the T-junction with the B5284 by The Sun PH in Crook turn left, then first right.

11 A steep climb with views towards High Street to the north, and the central fells to the west. Keep bearing left, ignoring turnings to the right.

12 Turn right at the T-junction with the B5284 ★ then immediately after the Golf Clubhouse, on the left, turn right signposted 'Heathwaite'. At the T-junction turn right into Lickbarrow Road.

13 At the crossroads at the end of Lickbarrow Road turn right. At the crossroads at the end of Park Road go straight ahead into Holly Road. At the T-junction with Ellerthwaite Road turn right. At the T-junction with the main road turn right to return to the start.

✚ Link To link with ride no 11, turn first right signposted 'Cartmel, Grange' This will give you a 56-km (35-mile) loop

★ Alt For a good quality off-road alternative back into Windermere, turn right at the T-junction with the B5284 then take the first right onto a no through road signposted 'Windermere, Dales Way'. Go through several gates. At the T-junction with a tarmac track turn left. At the T-junction with a lane turn right.

Dry-stone walls create a chequerboard of green fields

11 North of Cartmel

Another ride situated in the dense and complicated network of tiny quiet lanes east of Lake Windermere that make ideal year-round cycling. Cartmel is a real delight with its priory, old arches and buildings, attractive square and myriad refreshment possibilities. The first few miles out of Cartmel may be busier than the rest but after Lindale you escape into the charming lanes along the bottom of the valley formed by the River Winster. A steady climb to High Newton is rewarded with fine views across to Whitbarrow and down to Morecambe Bay.

1 From the centre of Cartmel take the road east towards Grange-over-Sands, then take the first left after the Priory. At the T-junction by the Pig and Whistle PH turn left. Continue for 2 kms (1.25 miles).

2 Take the first road right signposted 'Lindale 2½, Kendal 15'.

3 Go beneath some power lines and take the first right at the crossroads signposted 'Lindale via A590'. Climb the hill and continue for 1.2 kms (0.75 miles).

4 Take the first right. Continue climbing.

5 At the T-junction with the B5271 turn right then first left. Go past the Royal Oak PH in Lindale then shortly after the Post Office on a descent take the first left, just before Elmdale Inn. Continue for 4 kms (2.5 miles).

GRADE medium

DISTANCE 17 kms (10.5 miles)/28 kms (17.5 miles) with a link to ride no 10, Windermere Lanes

TIME allow 1.75 hours/2.5 hours

MAP OS Landranger 97 Kendal to Morecambe

GRID REF AT START 377787

PARKING carpark in Cartmel, follow the parking signs

TRAINS nearest stations Grange-over-Sands and Cark and Cartmel

TERRAIN woodland, farmland, river valley, low lying fells

SEASONAL SUITABILITY all year

SURFACE tarmac

CLIMBS/DESCENTS 1 long and 1 shorter climb

REFRESHMENTS full facilities, Cartmel; The Royal Oak PH, Elmdale Inn, Lindale; The Crown PH, High Newton; Hare & Hounds, Bowland Bridge just off the route at direction no. 9; Masons Arms, Strawberry Bank just off route

6 Turn right at the crossroads signposted 'Witherslack'◆. Go up and over a small hill.

7 Cross over the River Winster and bear left by triangle of grass. Go through the gates and continue for 4 kms (2.5 miles) through farm buildings at Askew Green.

An old stone arch in Cartmel

11 In High Newton, at the crossroads with the A590, go straight ahead, take care. At the T-junction opposite The Post House turn left, then turn first right signposted 'Barber Green'. After 0.8 kms (0.5 miles) turn left at the crossroads by a triangle of grass and continue for 1.2 kms (0.75 miles).

12 At the T-junction after the church, turn left signposted 'Cartmel'. Ignore two right turns, then after passing a left turn signposted 'Field Broughton', take the next right. Ignore the first left by power lines. Go past Broughton Grange.

13 Take the next left signposted 'Wood Broughton'. Continue for 1.6 kms (1 mile).

14 At the fork bear right. At the T-junction turn left signposted 'Cartmel' to return to the start.

8 At the T-junction bear left then go through a cluster of old buildings at Pool Bank. Continue for 1.2 kms (0.75 miles).

9 Turn first left by a triangle of grass signposted 'Bowland Bridge'✚ then turn first left again signposted 'Cartmel, Grange' (go straight ahead to visit the pubs at Bowland Bridge or Strawberry Bank).

10 Climb steadily, with a few short steep sections, for 7.25 kms (4.5 miles) following signs for High Newton.

◆ **SC** Turn left at the crossroads signposted 'High Newton'. There is a very steep push for 1.2 kms (0.75 miles). At the T-junction at the top bear left and rejoin the main route near direction no. 11.

✚ **Link** To link with Windermere Lanes do not turn left by the triangle of grass but continue straight ahead, joining the Windermere ride at direction no. 6.

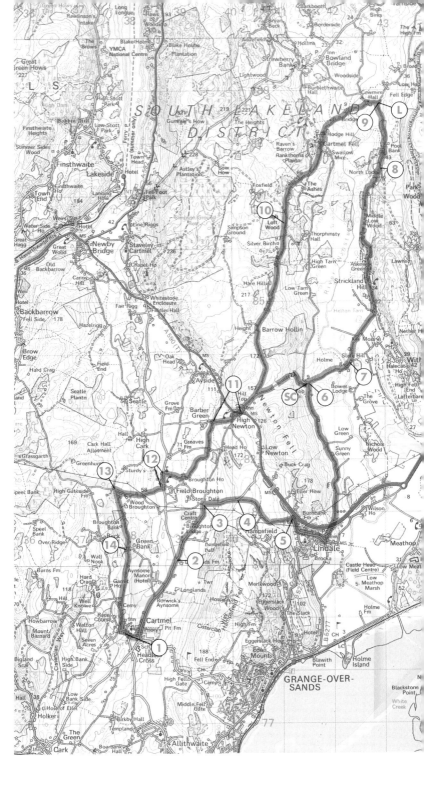

12 Quiet lanes west of Derwent Water

The network of lanes that lie between Derwent Water and the Derwent Fells take you through an area of dry stone walls, small green fields full of buttercups and hillsides carpeted with fern and foxgloves.

1 Follow the no through road to the end, dismount to cross the footbridge over the River Derwent. After the Derwent Water Hotel, at the T-junction in Portinscale, turn left signposted 'Grange'. Follow this road for 1.6 kms (1 mile).

2 Take the first road right signposted 'Ullock'.

3 Turn right at the T-junction signposted 'Braithwaite'◆. Cross the bridge over Newlands Beck and climb a short steep hill.

4 At the T-junction turn sharply left signposted 'Newlands, Buttermere'. Continue for 3 kms (2 miles). Turn right here for the Coledale Inn signposted 'Braithwaite'.

5 ◆ Continue straight ahead towards the distinctive lump of Rigg Screes and shortly after a sharp left-hand bend take the next left by Rigg Beck House signposted 'Newlands Church, Little Town'. Continue for 2 kms (1.25 miles).

GRADE medium	
DISTANCE 14.5 kms (9 miles) with a 9.5-km (6-mile) side trip to Grange	
TIME allow 1.5 hours for the loop, 1 extra hour to Grange	
MAP OS Landranger 89 West Cumbria/90 Penrith & Keswick/Outdoor Leisure 4 North West Lakes	
GRID REF AT START 255238	
PARKING no through road: on the B5289 heading out of Keswick towards Cockermouth, 400 m (440 yds) after last houses, take first no-through road to the left.	
TERRAIN fells	
SEASONAL SUITABILITY all year	
SURFACE tarmac	
CLIMBS/DESCENTS 1 main climb	
REFRESHMENTS pubs, Portinscale and Swinside; teashop, Grange; off route, Coledale Inn, Braithwaite; Lingholm Gardens (teas).	

6 At the crossroads turn right signposted 'Skelgill, narrow gated road'.

7 Go through the gate between two houses. At the T-junction with a more major road on a U-bend turn left signposted 'Portinscale, Keswick'★.

8 If you wish to visit the the Swinside Inn take the next left after 1.2 kms (0.75 miles). Otherwise follow the road back to Portinscale.

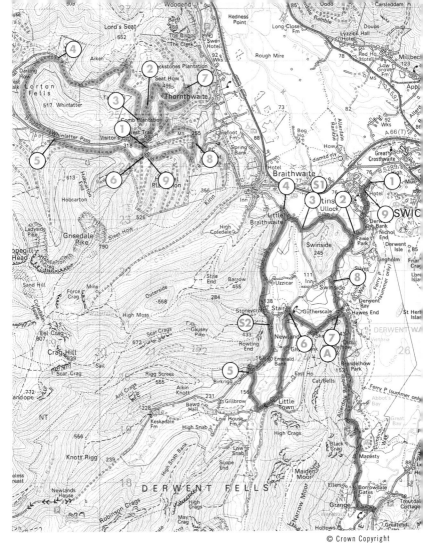

© Crown Copyright

9 On a sharp left-hand bend in Portinscale by Harney Park House turn right onto a no through road signposted 'Footpath to Keswick'. Dismount to cross the footbridge over the River Derwent to return to the start.

◆ SC1 Turn left at this T-junction signposted 'Swinside' and rejoin the route at direction no. 6.

◆ SC2 Take the first proper road to the right signposted 'Stair, Portinscale, Grange'. Rejoin the route at direction no. 6.

★ Alt turn right here signposted 'Grange'. Follow signs for Portinscale on the way back to join the main route at direction no. 7.

13 Whinlatter Forest

Waymarked long and short loops through the fourth of the forest rides through Whinlatter Forest Park.

Long loop

1 From Whinlatter Visitor Centre climb on tarmac towards the coach park and bear left onto a broad track near signpost no.15.

2 At the T-junction at the top of the climb turn left at signpost no.1 (purple bike sign).

3 At signpost no. 2, with the looming mass of Grizedale Pike and its signboard ahead, turn sharp right following the purple bike sign. This is a steep section. Descend over 2.5 kms (1.5 miles) with wide bends.

4 Go through the gate. On the next part of the descent, at signpost no. 27, bear left (purple bike sign). This is easily missed.

5 A long, grassier descent over 2.5 kms (1.5 miles). At the T-junction with the road turn left, then shortly right, and then left by signpost no. 32.

6 Go past the bike hire centre, descend to the road, turn left, then first right to return to the Visitor Centre.

GRADE medium	

GRADE medium

DISTANCE 11 kms (7 miles) long loop/8 kms (5 miles) short loop

TIME allow 1.5 hours long loop/1 hour short loop

MAP OS Landranger 89 West Cumbria or Landranger 90 Penrith & Keswick/Outdoor Leisure 4 North West Lakes

GRID REF AT START 208245

PARKING Whinlatter Visitor Centre, on B5292, west of Keswick

TERRAIN steep forested hills

SEASONAL SUITABILITY all year

SURFACE good quality forestry tracks

CLIMBS/DESCENTS many climbs and descents

REFRESHMENTS full facilities, Whinlatter Centre; Coledale Inn, Braithwaite

Short loop

1 From Whinlatter Visitor Centre climb on tarmac towards the coach park and bear left onto a broad track near signpost no.15.

2 At the T-junction at the top of the climb turn right at signpost no.1 (orange bike sign).

7 A steep climb is followed by a short descent. At a fork of tracks bear right downhill on a long descent over 2 kms (1.25 miles).

8 Go straight ahead at the road onto a steep single track, then turn left at the T-junction with a broad forestry track.

9 Follow the orange bike signs past the bike hire centre. At T-junction with the road turn left, then right to return to the Visitor Centre.

14 Coniston Water

A long descent to High Nibthwaite is the highlight of this ride with magnificent views of the lake with its yachts, steamers and windsurfers, and of Woodland Fell and back to the Old Man of Coniston.

1 Start at Grizedale Forest Visitor Centre. Turn right out of the carpark. Immediately after the Forestry Enterprise offices turn right onto the tarmac lane signposted 'Bike Route. Moor Top 2.8 miles, High Cross 5.2 miles'. As the road swings sharp right bear left over the cattle grid onto the blue bike-route track.

2 Climb steadily for 300 m (330 yds). Go through the bridgelate by a second cattle grid and turn sharply right uphill still on the blue bike route. After 300 m (330 yds), at the next blue bike route marker turn left sharply uphill onto a single track. Climb steeply for 0.8 kms (0.5 miles).

3 At the crossroads with 'No cycling' signs to right and left, go straight ahead.

4 At the next crossroads with 'No cycling' signs to right and left, go straight ahead onto a rougher stone track.

5 At the T-junction with a broader track turn right, then left by 'No cycling' sign ahead.

GRADE	medium
DISTANCE	18 kms (11 miles)
TIME	allow 2.5 hours
MAP	OS Landranger 96 Barrow-in-Furness or 97 Kendal to Morecambe
GRID REF AT START	335944
PARKING	Grizedale Forest Visitor Centre. From Hawkshead follow signs for the ferry, then pick up signs for Grizedale; from Newby Bridge, follow the A590 to Haverthwaite and turn right at the crossroads for Grizedale
TRAINS/FERRY	nearest station Windermere then ferry from Bowness
TERRAIN	lakeside, forestry, open moorland and farmland
SEASONAL SUITABILITY	late spring to late autumn
SURFACE	mainly tarmac, good forestry track, one boggy section
CLIMBS/DESCENTS	2 climbs/1 long descent
REFRESHMENTS	snack bar/restaurant, Grizedale Forest Visitor Centre; teas, Brantwood House; off route pubs in Coniston and Lowick Bridge

The descent to High Nibthwaite

© Crown Copyright

6 Follow carefully! At a fork of tracks by a large triangle of grass with trees growing in it, bear left, then at the crossroads with a major track go straight ahead and immediately right onto a narrow track. 'No cycling' signs tell you where you can't go. The track is rough for 1.2 kms (0.75 miles).

7 By the first isolated farmhouse, at a fork of tracks, ignore the grass track to the right and stay on the upper, left-hand track. Continue for 5 kms (3 miles) on a gently descending track, with short technical sections.

8 At the T-junction with the road turn right and follow the lakeside lane for 8 kms (5 miles).

9 This is easily missed: go past Brantwood House, on the right, and Low Bank Ground Outdoor Education Centre, on the left. Opposite the Bank Ground Farm B&B, turn right onto a broad stone track signposted 'Bridleway'. Go through the gate, then at the T-junction turn right signposted 'Satterthwaite, Grizedale'.

10 Climb/push up a steep track for 0.8 kms (0.5 miles). At a fork of tracks stay on the lower right-hand track.

11 After a long climb for over 0.8 kms (0.5 miles), bear right at the T-junction. At the second T-junction bear right.

12 Shortly after the brow of the hill ignore the first track to the left and after 50 m (55 yds) take the second track. Shortly after bear left at the next fork, a 'No cycling' sign is for the right-hand fork.

13 A semi-technical descent for 1.6 kms (1 mile) leads to a T-junction with wide forest track, turn right on the blue bike route. Ignore the first track left by a multicolour waymark and take the next left sharply back on yourself, following the blue bike route over the cattle grid back to the start.

15 Greystoke

Views to Blencathra, Great Dodd and across Ullswater are spectacular on this route. Greystoke is an attractive village, parts of it dating from the 17th century, and it boasts the impressive Greystoke Castle.

GRADE	medium
DISTANCE	24 kms (15 miles)
TIME	allow 2 hours
MAP	OS Landranger 90 Penrith & Keswick
GRID REF AT START	440308
PARKING	car park in Greystoke, just beyond the pub on B5288 towards Penrith
TRAINS	nearest station, Penrith
TERRAIN	open pasture
SEASONAL SUITABILITY	all year
SURFACE	tarmac
CLIMBS/DESCENTS	3 climbs/3 descents
REFRESHMENTS	Boot & Shoe PH, Greystoke; Saddleback Bar, Whitbarrow Leisure Village; Sportsmans Inn, just before the A66; pubs off route at Watermillock, Dacre and Penruddock

Looking over Ullswater to the central fells

1 With your back to the Boot & Shoe PH in Greystoke bear left signposted 'Berrier'.

2 Follow the long straight road ahead for 3 kms (2 miles). At the T-junction turn left signposted 'Troutbeck, Keswick'. At the next T-junction, by the Sportsmans Inn, turn left signposted 'Penrith (A66)'.

3 At the bottom of the hill turn first right signposted 'Matterdale'. At an offset crossroads with the A66 go straight ahead signposted 'Matterdale', take care. ◆

4 Ignore left turnings to Thackwaite and the drive to Brownrigg Farm. On a gentle right-hand bend take the next road left signposted 'Dockwray, Ullswater'. This is easily missed. A long climb for 2.5 kms (1.5 miles) is followed by a fast descent.

5 After descending for 0.8 kms (0.5 miles) by a green caravan sign take the first left signposted 'Single track road'. This is easily missed. Go past a telephone box and a campsite. Ignore the first left to Greystoke and the track on the left which is a dead end.

6 After 135 m (150 yds) bear left uphill on the next road, just before the start of a fast descent. Follow for 1.6 kms (1 mile).

7 At the T-junction turn left. At the crossroads turn right signposted 'Penruddock'.

8 At the crossroads with the A66 go straight ahead signposted 'Penruddock', take care. Continue for 3 kms (2 miles).

9 At the T-junction with the B5288 bear right signposted 'Greystoke, Penrith' to return to the start.

◆ SC For a short cut, take the next left after crossing the A66 signposted 'Stoddah, Hutton'. Bear right in Hutton, then at the T-junction turn left and rejoin at direction no. 8.

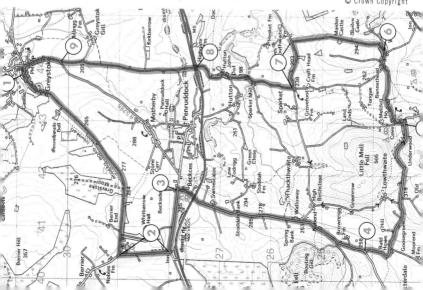

16 Askham Fell

Set in the northeast corner of the National Park, this ride has all the ingredients one might ask from an off-road ride in the lakes: a good starting point at Pooley Bridge, magnificent lakeside scenery, some tough climbing sections and a fast descent to finish.

GRADE medium

DISTANCE 14 kms (8.5 miles)/22.5 kms (14 miles)

TIME allow 2 hours/3 hours

MAP OS Landranger 90 Penrith & Keswick/Outdoor Leisure 5 North East Lakes

GRID REF AT START 472245

PARKING carparks in Pooley Bridge

TRAINS nearest station, Penrith

TERRAIN lakeside lane, open fell

SEASONAL SUITABILITY late spring to late autumn

SURFACE mainly stone-based track, tarmac, short boggy section

CLIMBS/DESCENTS 2 main climbs/2 descents

REFRESHMENTS pubs and teashops, Pooley Bridge; Helton Inn, Holywell Country Guest House (afternoon teas), Helton; Queens Head PH, Punch Bowl PH, Askham

1 With your back to the Swiss Chalet Inn in Pooley Bridge turn right on the B5320 towards Penrith. Immediately after the church take the first road right signposted 'Howtown, Martindale'. At the crossroads turn right onto a no through road signposted 'Howtown, Martindale'.

2 Go past the yacht club and the Sharrow Bay Hotel. Continue for 5.5 kms (3.5 miles). Shortly after the pier, at the end of this 'bay' on Ullswater, turn left onto a drive signposted 'Howtown Hotel'. This is easily missed.

3 Go past Howtown Hotel, pass between some buildings and start climbing, signposted 'Authorised vehicles only'. At a fork bear left up a gravel drive towards the house, signposted 'Mellguards.' Then bear left through a bridlegate marked with a blue arrow.

4 Take the right-hand track at a fork signposted 'Bridleway to Pooley Bridge', do not go through the gate to the left.

5 After a slate sign marked 'Divock Moor, Helton' the gradient steepens. Follow the track past a stone water tank set into the hillside, through a couple of boggy sections and follow a wood, then a stone wall to the left.

6 Follow the cairns (piles of stones), aiming to the right of the rounded hill crowned with a clump of trees, ahead. The path is vague beyond the stone circle called the Cockpit. At a bridleway crossroads turn left signposted 'Pooley Bridge' to return to the start on the short route. For the longer route, turn right signposted 'Helton'.

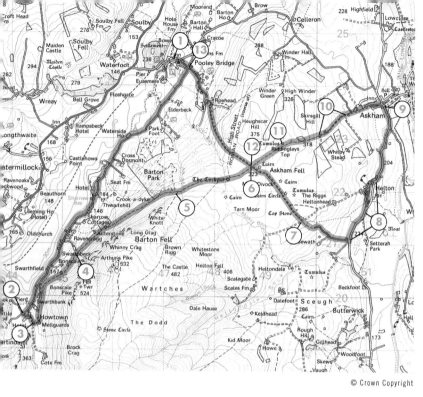

7 At the road go straight ahead signposted 'Bridleway, Bampton'. This soon becomes an enclosed track.

8 At the T-junction with a road turn left, then first left towards the Helton Inn ,and Helton village. Go through the village and at the T-junction at the end, turn left. Continue for 1.6 kms (1 mile) into Askham.

9 In Askham, opposite the Queens Head PH and the village stores, turn left.

10 At a fork of tracks soon after the cattle grid and houses, bear right onto a gravel track. As the main track swings left towards a conifer plantation, bear right (straight ahead) towards a copse of deciduous trees and a gate in the stone wall ahead.

11 Aim for the left hand edge of the wood. At the far corner of the wood bear slightly left downhill onto a more obvious track, parallel to the one you were following.

12 At the crossroads of bridleways turn right signposted 'Pooley Bridge'. This fast descent over 2 kms (1.25 miles) becomes tarmac.

13 At the crossroads go straight ahead signposted 'Pooley Bridge'. Then at the T-junction with the B5320, by the church, turn left to return to the start.

17 Eskdale

A gentle ride divided into two loops running beneath Muncaster Fell to the main road and crossing the River Esk which is tidal at this point. You may be able to smell the sea water. The route also runs parallel to the minature line of the Ravenglass and Eskdale Railway, known as the Ratty Line, and you will occasionally see the steam or hear the whistle of the train as it climbs up the valley to Dalegarth.

1 Starting at Dalegarth Station (labelled no. 12) continue west towards Eskdale Green. At the T-junction by the King George IV PH turn left signposted 'Ulpha, Broughton' and cross over the River Esk. The layby mentioned under **PARKING** (right) is on the right. 365 m (400 yds) after the bridge and just before the buildings of Forge Farm turn right onto a track signposted 'Bridleway, Muncaster Head Farm'. Follow this for 3 kms (2 miles), passing Muncaster Head Farm.

2 180 m (200 yds) after the track turns to tarmac, by the buildings of High Eskholme, leave the tarmac and bear left through the gate onto the lower track, signposted 'Main road' (blue arrow). Follow the track around the edge of golf course (marked by bridleway signs). Leave the golf course to the left of a golf green and go into woodland. This section may be muddy.

3 At the T-junction with a broad track turn right.

GRADE easy/medium	
DISTANCE 24 kms (15 miles)	
TIME allow 3 hours	
MAP OS Landranger 89 West Cumbria and Landranger 96 Barrow-in-Furness/Outdoor Leisure 6 South West Lakes	
GRID REF AT START 173007 Dalegarth Station car park/148995 layby on the road from Eskdale Green to Ulpha	
PARKING Dalegarth Station carpark or large layby near King George IV PH, Eskdale Green (*see* no. 1 left)	
TRAINS nearest station, Ravenglass	
TERRAIN riverside woodland, farmland, golf course	
SEASONAL SUITABILITY late spring to late autumn	
SURFACE mainly good, stone-based tracks, short rocky push and short boggy section	
CLIMBS/DESCENTS n/a	
REFRESHMENTS cafe, Dalegarth Station; King George IV PH, Eskdale Green; Woolpack Inn, Burnmoor PH, Brook House Hotel, Boot	

4 At the crossroads with a tarmac lane turn left – Eskdale Estate is signposted right. At the T-junction with the A595 turn left, continue for 1.2 kms (0.75 miles), cross the bridge and take the first road left signposted '6ft 6ins width limit'. Follow this lane for 5 kms (3 miles) with the River Esk to the left.

5 At the T-junction turn left signposted 'Eskdale Green, Whitehaven'. Continue for 1.2 kms (0.75 miles) to the end of the first loop. Just before the bridge over the River Esk turn right onto a track signposted 'Bridleway, Stanley Ghyll, Boot and Upper Eskdale'. Continue on the bank of the river for 1.2 kms (0.75 miles).

6 Take the right hand of two gates with a 'Bridleway' sign on it. The track is grassy and is followed by a short, stony section where you will have to push.

7 Go through mixed woodland. At the T-junction, with a stone wall and a house with ivy-clad round chimneys ahead, turn right.

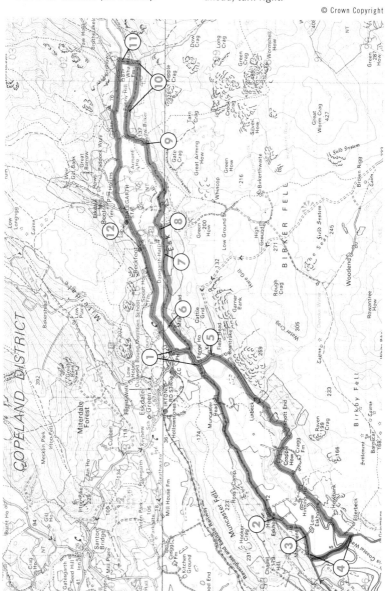

8 At the crossroads with a main track go straight ahead signposted 'Boot and Upper Eskdale'. Cross the wooden bridge over the first stream, ride through a second, smaller stream. Then there is a short climb. With a gap in the stone wall ahead, ignore the signpost straight ahead and bear right, following the track around the outside of the wall.

9 Cross the bridge over another small stream. At a fork of tracks, by house called 'Low Birker', bear left steeply downhill. At the T-junction with a tarmac track there is a hump-backed bridge to the left, turn right signposted 'Penny Hill Farm'.

10 Dismount going through the farm and follow the blue arrows. Continue for 1.2 kms (0.75 miles), cross another small stream and after 50 m (55 yds), at a three-way signpost turn left downhill through woodland. This is easily missed.

11 Negotiate a rough section through a field. Go through a gate onto a road and turn left over the bridge.

12 Follow this road for 3 kms (2 miles) back to the starting point at Dalegarth Station. It is 5.5 kms (3.5 miles) to the T-junction by the George IV PH, turn left signposted 'Ulpha, Broughton' for the layby.

18 Garburn Pass

Although graded difficult this ride does not demand advanced navigation skills, just a lot of energy and determination for the long climbs. The first is a 180 m (600 ft) climb to Stile End and you barely have time to recover before you start towards Garburn Pass. You may have to dismount and push on both the climbs, and on some of the descents, particularly the west side of Garburn.

GRADE	difficult
DISTANCE	35 kms (22 miles)
TIME	allow 4.5 hours
MAP	Landranger 90 Penrith & Keswick and Landranger 97 Kendal to Morecambe/Outdoor Leisure 7 South East Lakes
GRID REF AT START	470984
PARKING	Staveley village or if full park along the old road on the right going towards the A591 just before the main road
TRAINS	nearest station, Staveley
TERRAIN	woodland, farmland, high moorland
SEASONAL SUITABILITY	all year, take care on the two passes in winter
SURFACE	tarmac, rocky climbs dismount in places
CLIMBS/DESCENTS	2 tough climbs, 1 short climb/2 long descents, at times technical
REFRESHMENTS	teas and coffees, Stockdale Craft Centre halfway up Longsleddale (seasonal)

1 From the centre of Staveley take the road signposted 'Kentmere'. Go past the Wesleyan Chapel. After 300 m (330 yds) take the first road right signposted 'Burneside'. Follow for 4 kms (2.5 miles).

2 This is easily missed: ignore the first road left by a triangle of grass and a small concrete stand, go past Spring Hag, Hag Foot and Low Hundhowe and in a piece of woodland, shortly after a road sign for a left turn, take the next road left. (A signpost to 'Staveley' points back the way you have come). Follow for 3 kms (2 miles).

3 At the T-junction turn left signposted '6ft 6ins width limit'. Follow for 2 kms (1.25 miles).

4 Cross over the River Sprint in Garnett Bridge and turn left signposted 'Longsleddale' and follow the quiet dead-end lane up Longsleddale. Follow the tarmac to its end 6.5 kms (4 miles) ahead.

5 Bear left to cross the bridge where the tarmac turns to track. At the T-junction after the bridge turn left through farm buildings following the sign 'Byway to Kentmere'. Climb 180 m (600 ft) up and over Stile End pass.

6 At the T-junction with a tarmac track, turn left. Go through the gate and take the first road right sharply downhill.

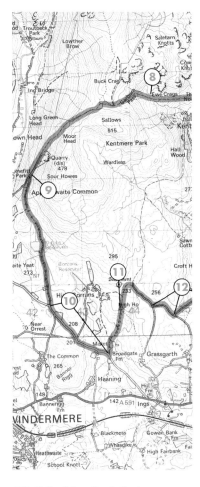

7 At the T-junction in Kentmere turn right and follow the tarmac lane to its end, passing to the left of the church.

8 Follow the signs for 'Byway, Garburn, Troutbeck' up a 280 m (930 ft) climb to Garburn pass, you will have to push most of the way.

9 Descending from Garburn Pass, some of the technical sections should be attempted by experienced riders only. At a fork of tracks bear left to go past Dubbs reservoir.

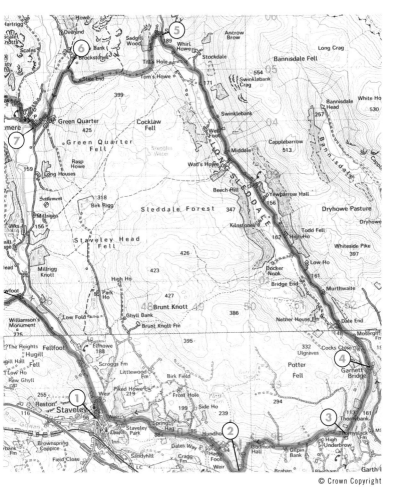

© Crown Copyright

10 At the road bear left. Ignore three right turns then 300 m (330 yds) after the third turn, near the bottom of a fast downhill stretch, just before the road starts climbing again and with a house and stone barn ahead, turn left signposted 'Bridleway to High House Farm'. This is easily missed.

11 At High House Farm follow the track to the right between a house and some barns. The track becomes grassier. Continue in the same direction with a wall to the right. At a gate turn right following the sign on the gate.

12 The track joins a better one. At a fork bear left. At a junction with a tarmac track and a bridleway/track straight ahead, turn left (GR 448004) downhill. Follow the river valley back down into Kentmere.

19 Woodland Fell to the Duddon Valley

This is a little-visited area of the National Park and offers some fine open riding away from the crowded central fells. It dips into the 'lost' valley of the River Duddon and has several tough climbs first to the foot of Dunnerdale Fells and then up a rocky track to the crags beneath Caw. The ride could easily be broken down into several shorter loops.

1 From the Wilsons Arms PH in Torver follow the A593 southwest towards Broughton-in-Furness for 0.8 kms (0.5 miles), then take the first road left by a cottage called 'The Crossings'. Continue for 2 kms (1.25 miles).

2 Go through several gates. At the end of the tarmac at the fork of roads/tracks bear right (straight ahead) on the lower, grassy track followed by a steep climb. Continue for 2 kms (1.25 miles). At the junction with a tarmac track, bear right. Go through lots of gates and ignore the first track to the left and the footpath soon after.

3 Take the second track left sharply back on yourself signposted 'Bridleway, Private Shooting'.

4 A steep then steady climb on gravel track over 0.8 kms (0.75 miles). At a fork bear to the right of the farm, the barn and through a bridlegate. Cross a stream and bear left uphill alongside the stream. Towards

GRADE difficult	
DISTANCE 40 kms (25 miles)	
TIME allow 5 hours	
MAP OS Landranger 96 Barrow-in-Furness	
GRID REF AT START 284942	
PARKING laybys along lane immediately after Wilsons Arms or ask to park in Wilsons Arms PH or Church House Inn carparks	
TRAINS nearest station Foxfield	
TERRAIN farmland, forestry, open fell and moorland	
SEASONAL SUITABILITY late spring to late autumn	
SURFACE tarmac, stone based track, boggy track	
CLIMBS/DESCENTS many climbs and descents, some severe	
REFRESHMENTS Blacksmiths Arms PH, Broughton Mills, Torver; Newfield Inn, Seathwaite	

the top of the climb fork right on the upper track. Short boggy sections follow. Descend for 1.6 kms (1 mile).

5 At the T-junction with a tarmac track bear right downhill.

6 At the T-junction turn right. The tarmac turns to track at Tottlebank. Follow for 1.2 kms (0.75 miles). The track turns back to tarmac at Birch Bank Farm.

7 A road joins from the left. At the T-junction with white lines across the end of your road turn right. A short climb then 1.6-km (1-mile) descent.

8 At the T-junction turn right over a cattle grid signposted 'Torver, Broughton'. At the fork 0.8 kms (0.5 miles) after the church bear left ◆ on the upper road then after a further 0.8 kms (0.5 miles) take the first road left signposted 'Broughton 3'.

9 At the T-junction with the A593 turn left, continue for 1.2 kms (0.75 miles) then, after a short steep section, turn right. At the T-junction with stone steps and a footpath ahead, turn left downhill. At the next T-junction with a green metal fence ahead turn right.

10 Go past the Blacksmiths Arms PH and the telephone box in

The open road over Subberthwaite Common

Broughton Mills. Cross the bridge and immediately bear left (straight ahead) onto the No Through Road. At Greenbank Farm bear right steeply uphill on the track furthest to the right. At the cottage turn left.

11 Go steeply uphill along the edge of woodland, through a gate and alongside a wall past a picnic table. Sea views are to the left. Stay on the track which runs between stone walls.

12 Follow this carefully. The route heads generally northwest and drops into the Duddon Valley but at times it may be vague and vary direction between southwest and northwest. Pass a stone and slate barn, 180 m (200 yds) further on ignore a bridlegate to the left and continue straight ahead uphill on a grass/stone track through bracken. At a fork at the col bear left downhill into the wooded valley below.

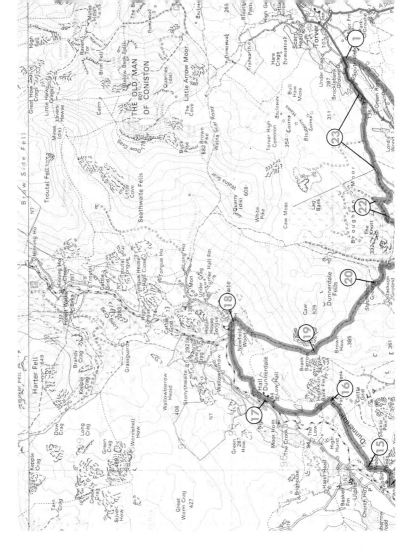

13 Shortly after two large outcrops of rock the path swings right to descend steeply through bracken to the road. There is a short boulder strewn section where streams cross the path. Soon after this keep an eye out for a track to the left which takes you directly down to the road. At the road turn right and continue for 1.6 kms (1 mile).

14 Soon after passing a left turn to Whistling Green, before a cluster of buildings on the right, take the track right signposted 'Bridleway, Private Road - No Turning'. This is easily missed, if you cross the river you have gone too far.

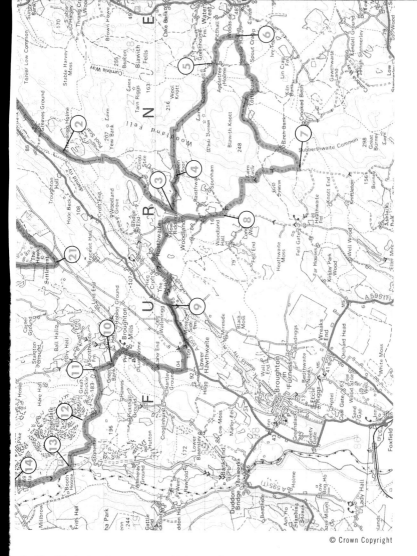

© Crown Copyright

15 Climb steeply on tarmac which turns to track beyond the gate by the house. Go through the wood on a good track. Leaving the wood bear right uphill on a stony track alongside a wall.

16 Follow the track past Kiln Bank Farm. At the road bear left ◆ downhill over the cattle grid down to the River Duddon.

17 At the T-junction by the telephone box bear right signposted 'Seathwaite, Wrynose'. Continue for 1.2 kms (0.75 miles).

18 50 m (55 yds) past the Newfield Inn, on sharp left-hand bend, take the middle of three gates signposted 'Bridleway'. It is a steep stony climb, joining a stream after 1.6 kms (1 mile).

19 Towards the top, where the stream you have been following crosses the path, leave the main track and bear left alongside the stream. After 90 m (100 yds) bear left uphill towards the crags to join a parallel, broader, grass tractor trail. As it swings left uphill bear right by stone cairns to follow the valley downhill.

20 The track is rough and boulderstrewn but soon improves. Go through a gate and follow a walled track. Go through a gate by a farm onto a tarmac track and bear left. Cross the bridge over a stream, descend on the road for 1.6 kms (1 mile).

21 Just before a second stream, turn left into the forest signposted 'The Hawk'.

22 Ignore the first narrow track to the right which goes alongside the stream. A major track joins from the left. Take the next track right signposted with a blue arrow. Cross the stream and climb for 0.8 kms (0.5 miles). At the T-junction with a wider forestry track turn sharply right and follow this main track as it swings in a wide arc round to the left and climbs to the road.

23 At the T-junction with the road turn left. Descend steeply for 1.6 kms (1 mile). At the T-junction with the A593 bear left to return to Torver.

◆ **SC1** After the church bear right and retrace the route between directions 2 and 1.

◆ **SC2** Turn right steeply uphill at the road, then after 5 kms (3 miles) turn left by the Blacksmiths Arms PH in Broughton Mills signposted 'Torver'.

Written by: Nick Cotton
Editor: Melanie Sensicle
Location photography: Nick Cotton
Designed by: Martin Lovelock
Production manager: Kevin Perrett
Managing editor: Miranda Spicer
Project manager: Kevin Hudson

Front cover photograph: Nick Cotton

First published 1995
© Haynes Publishing 1995

Published by:
Haynes Publishing
Sparkford, Nr Yeovil, Somerset BA22 7JJ

British Library Cataloguing-in-Publication Data:
A catalogue record for this book is available from the British Library.

ISBN 1 85960 115 4

Printed in Great Britain